Practical Business Communication

Practical Business Communication

Emma Sue Prince

First published 2017 by
PALGRAVE

Palgrave in the UK is an imprint of Macmillan Publishers Limited, registered in England,
company number 785998, of 4 Crinan Street, London, N1 9XW.

Palgrave® and Macmillan® are registered trademarks in the United States, the United
Kingdom, Europe and other countries.

ISBN 978–1–137–60605–1   paperback

This book is printed on paper suitable for recycling and made from fully managed and
sustained forest sources. Logging, pulping and manufacturing processes are expected to
conform to the environmental regulations of the country of origin.

A catalogue record for this book is available from the British Library.

A catalog record for this book is available from the Library of Congress.

Printed in China

Contents

Introduction

Rethinking contemporary business communication

The world of work you are entering now is a very different landscape from the one your parents will have gone into. Gone are the days when work followed a predictable 'escalator' where you completed school, got some qualifications, went to university (probably either for free or at a very low cost), got some experience, maybe went travelling for a while and then got your first job. Compared with now, until only a few years ago the world of work was relatively stable, predictable and the escalator flowed more or less smoothly to the top. Now, we need to, and have to, find ways to 'unjam' this escalator. Actually, let me rephrase that – you will find ways to do this. You're about to head into the most challenging labour market in 80 years.

Paradoxically and ironically, perhaps, many of you will have spent your school and university years preparing to be 'outstanding': you may have enjoyed music and sports activities, volunteered for various causes, even have travelled to exotic places. If you had any kind of learning challenges or difficulty, these are likely to have been recognised: you would have received support, standardised tests and extra time for examinations. Your school reports will, most likely, have been positive. The framework of school and university would have been clear and predictable. In most cases your parents will have supported and helped you with schoolwork and developing your unique potential.

You are also joining many others who, like you, will also have worked hard for their degree and qualifications. It's crowded out there and competition for work is fierce. But you have one key skill that is within your grasp and which you can discover and continue to develop now. It is key to propelling you towards the future you desire and to helping you achieve your very best. The best thing about this skill is that it is inside you and entirely within your control.

In today's knowledge economy and in your future work role, it is highly likely that you will be paid for your thinking skills rather than your doing skills. Information overload, diversity and a globalised workplace mean that **effective business communication skills** are more important than ever before because strong relationships forged by effective communication are the only currency we have and they are also our competitive advantage. Everything else can be copied and even the skills and knowledge you've worked so hard to attain at university and in higher education are easily replicated.

Our world is changing. According to leading futurist John B. Mahaffie and based on what is emerging and changing right now, we can say that:

- Our home lives and work lives will continue to be swept by regular waves of change. We need to be adaptable and resilient to manage change well and respond in ways that will benefit us, our families and our working lives.
- More work will involve international connections and citizenship will gain a more global focus. Therefore, we need to build our skills of empathy and interpersonal relationships.
- More work will be multidisciplinary, involving new kinds of collaboration. Confidence, working well with others, creativity and fast decision making will be key to working smartly and effectively.
- Far more jobs will mean working intimately with digital machines and intelligent systems. We need to embrace this and learn the skills we need to continue to be employable and add value as well as invent new products and services. In terms of skills this means creativity, problem solving and a lifelong commitment to learning.
- More elements of work and life will use visual communications because the way people consume their information is changing dramatically each and every day. There is already a high increase in media such as blogging, live-tweeting and video streaming and these are set to rise. We need stronger communication skills, including empathy, that embrace the new ways we communicate online and help us to do it more effectively.
- Visual and succinct communication is also important because of the huge increase in data. In fact, managing large volumes of data and multiple distractions requires organisation, prioritisation and multitasking skills that everyone needs to acquire and that are a key part of life skills.
- Citizenship responsibilities will only grow more complicated as societies confront new issues. That means developing the right expertise, self-awareness and experience to make a positive contribution and communicate effectively.

All of these areas influence the way we communicate, how we communicate and the skills and awareness we use to communicate.

Because we are operating in such a fast-moving environment we have become more prone to not working well and to communicating less effectively. This has an impact on how our brains process information and how we interpret cues from our environment. How we communicate has changed in the last three to five years and will continue to change as the pace of information and technology becomes faster and faster.

We seem to be getting worse at processing information and interpreting environmental cues – both important factors when it comes to communicating effectively. Quite often we are not sufficiently aware of these factors and our automated response mechanisms, which means we are not able to control or override initial reactions and responses, resulting in sub-optimal communication skills both in our personal and our work lives. One way to communicate better is having a stronger awareness and understanding of how our brain works, how it processes and interprets information and how to rise above our inbuilt automated responses and truly activate our brains for the better. Making complex decisions and solving problems effectively require a lot of brain energy and doing this is difficult for any length of time. We need to understand some of the real biological limits on our brain because this is one of the best ways to improve mental performance.

We also need to be far more aware of how technology can impede effective communication and how to manage our use of technology so that it enables us to communicate better. We are inundated with information overload in an unprecedented way. We now live in a world where we are constantly faced with more and more information, on a daily basis, more than we can possibly process. We live in an over-communicated environment. There are so many unwanted messages bombarding us that often the ones we want or are actually important get lost in the noise. The average person can now communicate faster, with more people – without thinking – than ever before and this is only set to increase. Information has become disposable. Much of this information comes at us online but increasingly it is simply everywhere, whether at home or at work, whether we are working or wanting to work or needing to relax or reflect.

This book is intended to help raise your awareness of how the way we respond to and interpret our environmental cues impacts our ability to communicate well. If we understand better how our brain is reacting and responding we will become better at knowing how to slow down, process information more effectively and create stronger relationships and networks.

Remember, too, that many of the skills needed for a successful student career can translate effectively into what is needed for a successful career within an organisation so it is likely that you've been putting good skills into practice already. Skills such as managing your workload, conducting a piece of research, giving presentations, and managing or leading projects are all going to be put to good use when you are in the workplace. Other experiences related to your friends and relationships, health and wellbeing and your own understanding of your strengths and weaknesses are vital, too, for enhancing the self-awareness from which everything starts.

The first three chapters look at key neuroscience breakthroughs about how our brains work, how to work smarter and therefore more productively, and how to overcome the one thing that impedes most our ability to be in the moment and focus: distraction. The rest of the book takes different modes of communicating, whether face-to-face or online, and summarises quick facts and statistics about that communication medium, followed by typical thought processes that are going on and specific environmental cues that we are either failing to notice or overlooking, and why, before focusing on tips, techniques and templates to use. The final chapter takes a 'week in the life' of someone at work and how they might put some of this awareness into practice. Throughout the book there are tips and exercises you can try out.

How to use this book

The book has been written in such a way as to allow you to dip in and out of sections that interest you but you can also work through it chronologically, like you would a course, if you want to. The chapters in this book inevitably develop from one to another. However, each chapter is designed to be complete and self-contained, enabling you to pick up the book and make use of odd hours between other demands on your time.

To help you check your progress through the book you will come across specific questions and exercises:

Self-checks are usually short questions or exercises to test your understanding of what you have just read, or to find out what you know already, before reading on. Do try answering the questions for yourself, if you can, before moving on to the discussion section.

Try this will be something you can try out immediately with friends, family or in other communication situations. *Try this* is designed to heighten your awareness of how your brain responds and to try out easy ways to override reactionary behaviour.

Exercises are similar to *self-checks* and come towards the end of a chapter to heighten your understanding of the whole chapter.

Putting it into practice are longer exercises and suggestions to help you apply your knowledge and practise the skills and techniques you have learned. Sometimes there will also be shorter exercises in the middle of the chapter to get you to carry out some observations or do some research so make a note of these when you get to them to remind yourself of what to do or what to look out for in the next few days or weeks. Remember that much of what is discussed will truly come to life for you when you can identify some of the examples and ideas with what is happening in your own life.

I also recommend keeping a journal or diary to record your thoughts and behaviours, preferably on a daily basis. If you are able to do this, you will notice a more immediate change and impact.

My aim in writing this book has been to adopt a direct and accessible tone and style of writing which makes the reader's task as easy as possible. I also want you to be able to go and try out some of the ideas and exercises in your own life and I encourage you strongly to do this and to notice what is happening in different communication situations that you find yourself in. It is only in this way that we develop self-awareness and it is only with self-awareness that we can grow and change.

Learning should be fun – so have fun and enjoy it! The way in which human beings communicate has always been and will continue to be fascinating, no matter how much technology comes into play and even when we fall short of perfection, which I know I do every day.

Your Amazing Brain

What's in this chapter:

- Did you know? Facts and statistics about how our brains work
- Your brain and your emotions
- The communication process model
- Communication is a question of personal credibility
- The brain and communication – what you need to know
- How CBT (cognitive behavioural techniques) can help raise awareness
- The SCARF model
- So what? How you can use the information in this chapter to enhance your communication skills

Did you know?

Facts and statistics about how our brains work

The conscious mind:

- comprises 17% of brain mass but only controls 2–4% of your perceptions and behaviour;
- looks for patterns and objects that are familiar. Interestingly, the conscious mind also rejects patterns and objects that aren't familiar;
- is where your free will lives. This is the part of you that thinks and reasons, and it is also the part of you that will decide what kind of changes you need to make in order to live the type of life you want to experience;
- is under your control. No person or circumstance can force you to think about thoughts or ideas that you don't specifically choose.

The subconscious mind:

- is most of your brain mass and controls 96–98% of your perceptions and behaviours;
- is nonverbal. Your subconscious mind sees in pictures and patterns. Your subconscious mind actually believes as true every picture or image you send it;

- doesn't know truth from fiction. This part of your brain doesn't know the difference between an apple and a picture of an apple – or, for that matter, between reality and imagination – which is why it is so crucial to understand how our emotions and feelings work as they often dictate what happens next!
- directs sensory input. Your subconscious brain has to complete 400 billion operations per second (!) because it is constantly assessing sensory input and deciding what to do with all that information;
- is retrainable! If you have negative patterns of thinking, bad habits you want to change or an inability to move forwards in achieving your goals and dreams you can change that by training your brain to perceive things differently. Once an idea is chosen and consistently impressed and emotionalised into the non-conscious mind, perceptions and behaviours change to find and produce the desired result.

What impact do you think all this has on our communication skills? Our brains truly are amazing and we have a conscious choice about how we engage our brains which in turn leads to learning to think and behave more effectively no matter what situation we may be in. So the emerging science of the brain is a natural place to develop more effective strategies for improving our communication skills.

Your brain and your emotions

Communication is linked to our emotions. Communication is about more than just exchanging information. It is also about understanding the emotion and intentions behind the information. Effective communication is a two-way street, and not only how you convey a message so that it is received and understood by someone in exactly the way you intended, but also how you listen to gain the full meaning of what's being said and to make the other person feel heard and understood.

More than just the words you use, effective communication combines a set of skills including nonverbal communication, engaged listening, managing stress in the moment, the ability to communicate assertively, and the capacity to recognise and understand your own emotions and those of the person you're communicating with. This may sound only applicable to face-to-face communication but it is also very important for online communication, messaging and email.

The diagram below shows the classic communication process model (Shannon, 1948; Berlo, 1960; Weaver and Shannon, 1963; Schramm, 1964; Barnlund, 1970; Lanham, 2003).

Transmission phase

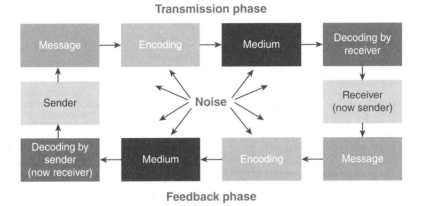

Feedback phase

Example: how the communication process model works

Lindsey is the supervisor of a team of employees in a research and development department for a small tech company that currently focuses on new apps. Her boss wants Lindsey to work on a new project. But Lindsey can't successfully manage her team in order to complete the project unless she is able to effectively communicate with them. Communication is the process of conveying information between two or more people. The communication process breaks down the steps we take in order to achieve a successful communication.

A sender is the party that sends a message. Lindsey, of course, will be the sender. She'll also need the message, which is the information to be conveyed. Lindsey will need to encode her message, which is transforming her thoughts about the information to be conveyed into a form that can be sent, such as words.

A channel of communication must also be selected, which is the manner in which the message is sent. Channels of communication include speaking, writing, video transmission, audio transmission, electronic transmission through emails, text messages and instant messaging and even nonverbal communication, such as body language. Lindsey also needs to know the target of her communication. This party is called the receiver.

The receiver, in this case her team, must be able to decode the message, which means mentally processing the message into understanding. If you can't decode, the message fails. For example, sending a message in a foreign language that is not understood by the receiver probably will result in decoding failure. Decoding failure also happens when the message is misinterpreted in some way. Of course every message sent is open to interpretation and to the receiver's perceptions so there is a lot of room for potential miscommunication to occur.

Sometimes, a receiver will give the sender feedback, which is a message sent by the receiver back to the sender. For example, a member of Lindsey's team may provide feedback in the form of a question to clarify some information received in Lindsey's message. Then the encoding process starts all over again. In this model, 'noise' is simply any type of disruption or distraction that interferes with the transmission or interpretation of information from the sender to the receiver.

Active listening, which requires focus, is key to successful encoding and decoding as well as overcoming any noise and lessening potential misinterpretation of our messages. Active listening underlines effective and productive conversations, meetings and probably any kind of communication process between people. Underlying each element of the communication process model, and determining how we interpret incoming information and control outgoing information, is the brain.

The brain and communication – what you need to know

This section aims to give you a brief guide to our brains in terms of communication. I am not intending to describe every part of how our brains work – that is not the purpose of this book – but rather to provide a basic understanding of what is going on and how that relates to the way we communicate.

The frontal lobe is the part of the brain that controls emotions, problem solving, memory, language, judgement and other skills, as well as social and sexual behaviour. It is, in essence, home to our personality and our ability to communicate. The frontal lobe is one of the four major divisions of the cerebral cortex. The cerebral cortex regulates decision making, problem solving, control of purposeful behaviours, consciousness and emotions, and is heavily connected with reasoning.

Think of the brain as a seesaw: on one side are the frontal lobes, the region associated with reasoning; on the opposite side is the amygdala, where emotions, both good and bad, are generated. In between, is the anterior cingulate, which mediates the opposing forces.

In each person, one side is inherently more influential than the other, according to neuroscientist Dr Andrew Newberg. What results is a person's temperament (an internal balance or emotional tone), which can shift further to one side or the other depending on external forces. These forces can be traumatic (a divorce or bereavement), annoying (traffic), or health related (poor-quality sleep, inadequate nutrition) – any of these forces can trigger chemical changes that compromise brain activity. For a hotheaded type, whose brain may already seesaw towards the emotional side, negative events can exacerbate imbalance. For an even-keeled personality, the brain may tip over to the emotional side only ever so slightly. In either case, if chemical changes are triggered this can mean the difference between a run-in with a colleague or friend that ruins your entire weekend and one that you can shrug off without a second thought or only minimal upset.

This is why self-awareness is so important when it comes to communication. If you are aware of your natural temperament and that there are things which may trigger it then there are strategies you can adopt to help you cope better. For example, there are very practical things you can do like ensuring you do have enough sleep and are getting the right nutrition as well as knowing that if you have slept badly you may be more prone to reacting negatively. If you know this, then doing something as simple as taking a deep breath or drinking a large glass of lemon-infused water first thing in the morning will help. Equally, if you know you are prone to being quite hotheaded and emotional you can start to use cognitive behavioural techniques (known as CBT) to help – an example is to be able to reason with yourself when something external happens. A situation you may find yourself in may cause unhelpful thoughts which in turn can easily lead to negative feelings. What a CBT technique will do is help you challenge these thoughts to turn them into something more solutions focused and positive as well as realistic. This uses the reasoning part of your brain and the more you do this the more you can strengthen this process. Doing this means that you will be in a much stronger position to respond more positively and not merely react to everything around you or presented to you.

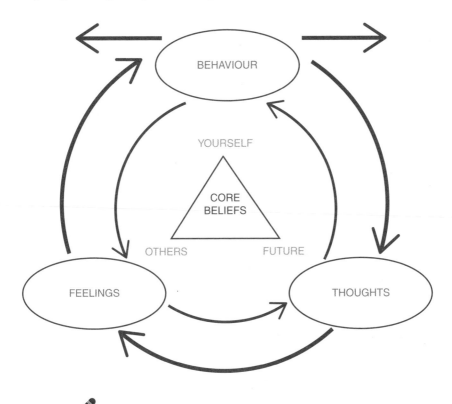

Try this

Example situation: You are tired and have had a busy day. When you get home, one of your family members or your flatmate seems angry and starts listing things you should have done. These are some ways your brain may respond and how you might start to positively influence these responses:

UNHELPFUL THOUGHTS – STOP
Remember these are thoughts that are going on inside you – you are not necessarily voicing them but they are there and will influence what happens next.

HELPFUL THOUGHTS – GO
Remember that this is you exercising a degree of control over your thoughts – you are not voicing them (as with unhelpful thoughts) but they are there and will influence what happens next.

He/she's always going on about this stuff and never does anything about it	It's probably true that there are things on this list that I could have got around to doing
Why do I always have to do everything around here?	S/he may have had a tough day too
This is terrible – I can't stand this kind of stress and I don't need this right now	I know I am feeling tired and a bit stressed – maybe I need to just take a deep breath and listen
Who does s/he think s/he is? A list? Really? What is this?	It's just a list – it's OK!
FEELINGS:	**FEELINGS:**
Anger	Things are OK
Upset	Calm
Stressed	Rational and in control
Annoyed	
BEHAVIOURS:	**BEHAVIOURS:**
Shouting in response (voicing the thoughts)	Listening in order to understand
Slamming everything down dramatically	Focusing, breathing, allowing the situation to be
Having a big argument about it	Having a look at the list together and seeing what can be realistically done and when
Eating a massive bar of chocolate to 'feel better'	
Complaining about the situation on social media to get validation of your feelings and behaviours	

Try this ✏

Think of a typical situation that might potentially upset you. Even better, can you anticipate something that might be coming up quite soon in your life? Write a few notes on this situation and then try to articulate the unhelpful thoughts you might have and the resulting feelings and behaviours. Then do the same with helpful thoughts.

Situation:

_____

_____

_____

_____

_____

_____

_____

_____

_____

_____

UNHELPFUL THOUGHTS – STOP	HELPFUL THOUGHTS – GO
Remember these are thoughts that are going on inside you – you are not necessarily voicing them but they are there and will influence what happens next.	_Remember that this is you exercising a degree of control over your thoughts – you are not voicing them (as with unhelpful thoughts) but they are there and will influence what happens next._
FEELINGS:	**FEELINGS:**
BEHAVIOURS:	**BEHAVIOURS:**

CBT is based on positive psychology techniques and on the idea that problems aren't actually caused by situations themselves (however tempting it is to give in to this idea) but instead by how we interpret the problem or situation in our thoughts. It is this that can then affect our immediate and subsequent feelings and actions. Because communication is a key way that we respond to problems or situations, using reasoning and CBT techniques can be a very effective way to change behaviour and have more positive communication as well as less stress! Remember the subconscious mind is retrainable and CBT or positive psychology exercises are great ways to do that. Give it a try by getting into the habit of questioning your own feelings and behaviours – you will notice a difference very quickly both in terms of your conversations and how much you feel in control.

The amygdala is in the unconscious brain. It's a small almond-shaped structure in what is called the 'limbic system' of the brain and it is responsible for many emotional reactions.

There are two main points to be aware of here:

1) The logical brain is able to override the emotional brain. For example, you can take a rational look at any situation and realise that you may be exaggerating the potential risks to yourself. For example, if you were asking for a favour you might come to the conclusion: 'The worst-case scenario is that the person I'm requesting something from says no – that's not the end of the world!' This thought will help you to be calmer, and build the confidence to actually make the request in the first place and perhaps even make it more effectively too. This can help if you were feeling nervous about making the request – perhaps the person is someone in authority or your perception of the request is that it is potentially a 'big ask'.

This kind of internal talking to yourself is very helpful and has an immediate effect, whereas if you do the opposite and start catastrophising a situation you will only create stress. Yet it is easy to catastrophise any situation and even easier when we hear others around us doing it too, i.e. 'that was a nightmare' or 'it was a total disaster' when merely referring to plans changing at the last minute or not having enough time to complete a project. The language we use to talk about any situation is very powerful and if we also use that language to publicly share on social media this only feeds the drama. You will find plenty of validation on social media and your brain will love this. However, it does not help handle a situation well and actually contributes to your stress levels considerably.

It can be quite hard to do this in the moment because catastrophising thoughts and using dramatic language can be quite automatic, but the more you increase your own awareness the easier it is to catch these thoughts before they take hold and to think twice before sharing them on social media platforms.

Try this ✎

Try and catch yourself – next time you are having a conversation about something, watch for when you might be using 'catastrophy' language and watch for when someone else might be using it. You will be surprised by just how often this occurs on a daily basis and it's important to remember that the more we use this kind of language and articulate our thoughts and feelings in this way the more our brain will believe it. Raise your awareness and start using more appropriate language for the situation at hand – it's not a disaster if your train is late and it's not a nightmare if you forgot to bring a key document to a meeting. The more you can do this and change the language you use the better you will feel and the quicker your brain will tap into its own resourcefulness to resolve the situation.

2) Every time the logical brain overrides the emotional brain, the logical brain 'muscle' becomes stronger and stronger. In other words, through CBT training

the brain actually reinforces the neural pathways, so it becomes easier and easier to deal with future stressful situations.

This links back to what we said earlier about training the brain which is why it's so important to be aware of your own natural inclination to jump to a particular conclusion or attach meaning to something. The more you can be aware of this and choose different behaviours the better your communication skills will become. It's not always easy, though, because you will find that people around you will be very happy to 'feed' your exaggerations or negative conclusions which is why it is so important to be mindful of how you talk about things, no more so than on social media.

First impressions

When you're dealing with people face-to-face, your facial expressions might be revealing more than you think!

The amygdala interacts with your prefrontal cortex to generate and process the main emotions of anger, happiness, disgust, surprise, sadness and fear. Your initial response to any situation will be rooted in one of these major emotions.

This is one of the reasons to become more aware of body language and facial expressions when you are communicating, both of which are not accessible with online communication. In face-to-face communication these initial responses and emotions are visually present for split seconds if we are observant enough to see them!

Managing 'noise'

Let's revisit the 'noise' element of the communication process. Managing this is an important element of communication because it relates to how messages are decoded and understood. Because how we perceive incoming information is subjective and open to misinterpretation we need to sharpen our focusing skills and our listening skills so that if we are on the receiving end of a message we are more able to understand it. This is where your working memory comes in. Think of it as your brain's scratch pad or sticky note. It holds new facts just long enough for you to problem solve and is critical to your ability to control your attention and to concentrate despite distractions. However, your working memory has limitations and is affected when you try to do too many things at once or are faced with an overload of information.

The SCARF model

The SCARF model is a helpful acronym that summarises the five domains of social experience that your brain treats the same as survival issues. Get a handle on these and you will be able to handle most communication situations with ease and grace as well as understand better your own responses to things.

The SCARF model was developed by Dr David Rock, and stands for Status, Certainty, Autonomy, Relatedness and Fairness.

The model describes the interpersonal primary rewards (or threats) that are the most important to the brain. Knowing, understanding and making use of this model can help you develop language for experiences that otherwise sit in your subconscious brain, so that you can catch these experiences as they are happening. All elements in the SCARF model are important but at any time even if just one of them is disregarded a lot of miscommunication can result.

S is for Status	Status is our sense of worth, it's where we fit into the hierarchy, and this can be both socially as well as related to work. Status is a significant driver of behaviour. If our sense of worth is threatened in any way, we are likely to react. Many everyday conversations become arguments driven by a status threat, a strong desire to not be perceived as less than another. In a communication situation status is increased through sharing important information, giving responsibility, praising and recognising and it's threatened by criticism, failure or feeling excluded from conversations.
C is for Certainty	Clarity and certainty are important to us. Our brain uses up fewer resources in familiar situations than unfamiliar ones. So communicating or working with a lack of clarity can increase stress levels and impair our ability to make effective balanced decisions. Certainty can be created through routine, clear and regular communication and short, direct messages. Certainty is threatened by change so the more clarity and information that can be given or sought after, the better.
A is for Autonomy	Autonomy gives us a sense of control over what we do and is linked to having choices in a situation. Our brain will process a lack of autonomy or choice as a threat situation (and this will lead to more stress), whereas being promised more autonomy actually activates the reward system in the brain. This is also about feeling in control of a situation.
R is for Relatedness	We're social animals, and we naturally form social groups and build relationships. These groups build mutual trust and form a barrier against the unknown. This leads to the production of oxytocin, which increases the positive feeling of trust and stabilises these relationships. This helps a lot if you are working in a team. Creating rapport is key to generating relatedness and can be as simple as shaking hands, using a person's name or chatting about personal interests. Deeper rapport can be achieved through active listening and demonstrating empathy.
F is for Fairness	If we think something is unfair, our brain automatically goes into defence mode. A strong response that removes the unfairness can activate the reward centre of the brain. If something seems unfair, it rapidly triggers intense emotions and the 'threat' response. It uses up a lot of mental energy and distracts from everything else.

The extent to which we feel something is a threat or a reward will determine our behaviour and our communication.

So, if we perceive something as a threat this has an immediate impact on our working memory (ability to problem solve and manage distraction), tends to narrow our view and generalise the threat and leads to greater pessimism. On the other hand, if we perceive something as a reward we will have improved access to our own cognitive resources and ability to problem solve, meaning we will get more insights and more ideas and make fewer perceptual errors.

Remember, these reactions are hard-wired into the brain and are not the result of our conscious choices. However, an emotionally intelligent, self-aware adult will have some capacity to suppress or manage the 'threat' response and generate their own 'reward' state. Being emotionally intelligent means that you have a strong sense of self-awareness about your own emotions and responses to events and other people and are able to self-manage these effectively.

What is emotional intelligence?

Emotional intelligence (EI) is the ability to identify and manage your own emotions and the emotions of others. It is generally said to include three skills:

1) Emotional awareness, including the ability to identify your own emotions and those of others;
2) The ability to harness emotions and apply them to tasks like thinking and problem solving;
3) The ability to manage emotions, including the ability to regulate your own emotions, and the ability to cheer up or calm down another person.

Its formal definition is 'the capacity for recognising our own feelings and those of others, for motivating ourselves and for managing emotions effectively in ourselves and in others. A learned capability that contributes to effective performance' (Goleman, 1999). The EI competencies fall into four categories: self-awareness; social awareness; self-management; and relationship management (or social skills).

This set of definitions was popularised by Daniel Goleman in his books *Emotional Intelligence, Working with Emotional Intelligence* and *The New Leaders*. One of the key EI competences for communication is emotional self-control; another is empathy. Others are self-confidence, transparency, organisational awareness, service orientation and influence. In simple terms, if you are going to be a good communicator, you need to be able to listen, control your personal expectations and preferences, be self-assured and speak in accordance with your values, understand and allow for the climate and culture within which you are speaking, engage with other people and anticipate the effect of your actions and words.

The SCARF model is important when it comes to communicating with others, especially in leadership or in team situations when you want to get the best out of people. If any one of the five components of SCARF is not taken fully into account the results are likely to be miscommunication, misunderstandings and defensive behaviour and these reactions can happen very quickly in others as well as in yourself.

Understanding the SCARF model can help you both minimise threats and maximise rewards inherent in everyday experience. For minimising threats, knowing about the domains of SCARF will help you to label and reappraise experiences that might otherwise reduce performance. Labelling (Lieberman et al., 2007) and reappraisal (Ochsner and Gross, 2005) are cognitive tools that have been verified in brain studies to be effective techniques for reducing the threat response.

Labelling means being able to voice the labels you are giving to your emotions. It raises awareness of the emotion and lessens the threat element of it. So you can say to yourself: 'I'm feeling angry', 'I'm feeling sad', 'I'm feeling not in control' or 'I'm feeling left out' – doing this helps your brain to figure out more appropriate responses in that moment and is instant if you can get into the habit of doing it!

Reappraisal means being able to reframe the situation or emotional stimulus and reinterpret it. When you do this, the emotions you experience lose a bit of their intensity and allow you to deal more productively with whatever triggered them in the first place. Let's say you are running late for a party and have taken a wrong turn. At first you may get frustrated and blame your satnav. Almost immediately you may experience negative thoughts such as 'I'm always getting lost, what's wrong with me?' and 'People will think I'm disrespectful for being late' and then before you know it you are angry and stressed and this affects your being able to enjoy the party fully when you get there. Reappraisal would mean you catching yourself in that downward spiral and nipping it in the bud by saying to yourself, 'Actually people aren't really going to care that much if I'm late' or 'I might as well enjoy the journey and I'll soon be back on track'.

This is simply an alternative way of dealing with the situation, allowing you to experience things more positively and achieve a different outcome as a result – i.e. being present and interacting with people at the party and enjoying yourself.

These techniques have been shown to be more effective at reducing the threat response than the act of trying to suppress an emotion (Goldin et al., 2007). Knowing about the elements of SCARF will help you to understand issues such as why you can't think clearly when someone has attacked your status, instead of just trying to push the feeling aside.

Knowing the domains of SCARF also allows you to design ways to motivate yourself more effectively. An example might be giving attention to increasing your sense of autonomy during a time of uncertainty, such as focusing on the thrill of doing whatever you like when suddenly out of work.

Try this ✎

Think of a recent situation where you experienced a misunderstanding with someone else or with a group of friends/colleagues. Looking back, are you able to identify elements of the SCARF model that may have been disregarded lurking behind the issues? Disregarding even just one element of SCARF can lead to misunderstanding.

What was the situation you experienced? Try to describe it and link it to one or more of the SCARF elements	Questions you could ask
Status	Was status threatened in any way – i.e. was someone's role or authority not acknowledged or disregarded? Remember, this could be simply a perception or could be the way something was communicated, even through body language. Or was there criticism of something or failure to recognise contribution or achievement? Was someone left out or excluded in some way?
Certainty	Was there sufficient clarity in communications? Did everyone understand what was going on? If asking others to do something, were there goals and specific guidelines?
Autonomy	Did people have a say in the decision or situation? Was there choice or did it feel there was 'no choice'? Were people entrusted to do something or carry out something specific and then allowed to get on with it?
Relatedness	Was there rapport? Did people use each other's names, pay attention to each other, listen? Or did the atmosphere feel charged with negative tension and disharmony?
Fairness	Did anything happen that might have been *perceived* as being unfair in some way? This could be as simple as not having a chance to speak or the perception that a decision or process has been unfair in some way.

Then think of a situation coming up where you need to communicate with a group or team. How can you ensure that all elements of the SCARF model are covered and how will you do this?

Description of the situation with a group or team where you could use the SCARF model	Things you can try
Status	Making sure everyone's status is maintained – do this by giving positive feedback, encouraging people's views and opinions, validating responses, listening, keeping everyone informed and involved and acknowledging people's roles and contributions.

(Continued)

Certainty	Having clear goals, strategies and plans and telling the group or team about them. Establishing routines for keeping people up to date and regular opportunities for them to contribute their own ideas.
Autonomy	Working as part of a team significantly reduces the perception of autonomy and can raise stress levels quite dramatically so make sure you create opportunities to include individuals' judgement and insight, and if you give someone a task to do let them decide how they are going to do it as long as the results are clear. Also make sure you are working with people you can trust; if you can't trust them start asking yourself why and work out how to increase trust.
Relatedness	Paying attention more, listening more, being encouraging and inclusive and using people's names.
Fairness	Each individual person has their own view of what is fair, but most people are also open to seeing a different version of fairness if it can be explained fully. So make sure you explain any potentially contentious decisions fully. As you talk people through the issues and the thought process you not only restore their sense of fairness, you also increase their status and feeling of relatedness at the same time, triggering a powerful 'reward' response in the face of what could have been seen as a threatening situation.

Five exercises to try:

All of these will improve your wellbeing fast and impact how you communicate, too.

1) Three funny things

Write down three funny things you experienced in a given day, and why those things happened. For example, was this something you were directly involved in, something you observed, or something spontaneous?

When you can laugh at yourself and your circumstances, it means that you don't take life too seriously and can keep things in a healthy perspective. Best of all, laughing is contagious!

2) Keeping a journal

Keeping a journal provides a snapshot of a moment in time. Not only does journalling create a healthy habit of self-reflection, it allows us to document positive changes to our thinking and our actions, and it helps transition from a bad mood to a good one. It also helps retrain our brain to create more positive behaviours because writing things down raises our awareness. See also Chapter 10 – *The Power of the Pen* for more on journal writing.

For example, if you did really well on a particular work or study assignment this week, you would recount:

How it happened (through hard work and spending 15 minutes double-checking headings and subheadings)

Why it happened (I had a clear work plan and made space in my schedule and I also used smart-working (more on this in Chapter 3 – *Working Smarter*) which made a big difference)

What I did right (I made sure I really understood what was expected in the assignment and the criteria for success)

How I helped this happen (I gave up watching my favourite TV shows and read up on all my notes and did some additional research instead)

Now try this: record one activity that you didn't like and how you can address it. For example:

I snapped at my roommate when she came home late on Thursday and woke me up.

Problem solve the following:

How this is keeping me stuck (I couldn't fall back asleep because I obsessed over how inconsiderate she is)

What thoughts and actions I can take to get unstuck (I can be more flexible; after all, she's a grown-up and doesn't need a curfew. I can buy earplugs and wear them when she goes out during the week)

Try it yourself – this may seem like a time-consuming exercise but it takes very little time and will raise your awareness *immediately* and will also impact how you communicate with others around you.

3) Count kindness gestures

Keep a record of all the kind acts that you do in a particular day, and the acts of kindness you witness. These can be as simple as cooking a meal for friends, helping an elderly person cross the street or smiling at strangers. Notice how doing these small things creates a 'feel-good' factor in your brain which is immediate.

4) Gratitude visit

Think of someone you could thank, someone who's been helpful or kind to you (and not necessarily a family member, partner or close friend). Write a letter to this person, including details about how they've helped you and the lasting impact this has had on you. Arrange to meet up with your friend and tell them you have something to read to them. After you finish reading the letter, present it as a gift.

A lovely gesture, though entirely optional, is to put the letter in a frame or to laminate it.

5) Cultivate a positive outlook

Despite the bad things that happen daily, it's important to remember that the world is basically a safe place.

We all suffer pain and trauma. People who look at the bright side of every situation possess the resilience to bounce back quicker. When you intentionally choose positivity, you look inwards for resources and you trust your thoughts, emotions and behaviours. Life still brings its challenges, but you know that you do have the tools to help you look at some of the alternatives open to you in that situation.

So what? How you can use the information in this chapter to enhance your communication skills

This chapter has focused on giving you some insight into how your brain works when it comes to communication skills.

Understanding a bit more about how your brain works is going to be a great asset when it comes to communicating effectively, whether you are writing, talking, presenting or messaging online. Getting a stronger sense of awareness about yourself and your, often automatic, responses to things can help you to retrain your brain to use more appropriate thoughts which in turn will lead to more effective behaviour and outcomes. The exercises give you small chunk-sized activities that you can hopefully easily incorporate into your everyday life and notice an immediate impact. By developing awareness, we are much better able to manage ourselves and look after ourselves well. Most of our communication skills are fully within our own ability to control and improve. Practising self-awareness helps you to feel and be more in control over your life and your ability and confidence to deal with situations and make decisions. Rather than resorting to 'flight' or 'fight' mode when we are asked to give a presentation or when someone sends us an abrupt email or doesn't act as we had expected, we can rise above those automatic reactions and choose a different response. We can recognise when we are tired or feeling stressed and do things that can help us. We can adopt routines and strategies that help us to live more fully and engage more fully and positively with the world around us.

Your communication skills are one of your most important and valuable assets.

Further reading

Brann, Amy. 2013. *Make Your Brain Work: How to Maximize Your Efficiency, Productivity and Effectiveness.* Kogan Page.

Cain, Susan. 2014. *Quiet: The Power of Introverts in a World That Can't Stop Talking.* Penguin.

Rock, David. 2009. *Your Brain at Work: Strategies for Overcoming Distraction, Regaining Focus, and Working Smarter All Day Long.* Harper Business.

How to Overcome Distraction

What's in this chapter:

- Did you know? Facts and statistics about distraction
- Why is distraction such a problem?
- Two core skills that help manage distraction and increase your productivity levels
- The discipline of focus
- The magic of being 'in flow'
- How overcoming distraction leads to greater productivity
- How to deal with distraction – tips and ideas
- So what? How you can use the information in this chapter to overcome distraction

Did you know?

Facts and statistics about distraction

A recent study on digital distraction, *The Cost of Interrupted Work: More Speed and Stress* (Mark, 2016), conducted by the Department of Informatics at the University of California, revealed the following:

- Once distracted it can take the average person 23 minutes to get back to the original task.
- The average amount of time that people spend on any single event before being interrupted or before switching to something else is about three minutes.
- 44% of the time people tend to interrupt themselves. The rest of interruptions come from external sources.
- The average person spends 13 hours a week (that's a full 28% of their work week) reading, deleting, sorting and sending emails.
- People who are very productive tend to spend a specific period of time on one task (i.e. 90 minutes) followed by a shorter time of rest before moving on to the next task.

Why has distraction become such a problem?

Why do we need to overcome distraction? Why has distraction become such a key issue and why is the ability to focus fast becoming a must-have skill? We are distracted today more than ever because day-to-day we are dealing with an overload of information, requests, demands and general 'busyness', much of our own making and which we feel compelled to react to. Our brain is not equipped to do tasks simultaneously. What we are really doing is just switching tasks quickly so each time we move from hearing music to writing a text or talking to someone, there is a start/stop/start process that goes on in the brain that uses up energy.

That start/stop/start process takes its toll on us in quite a negative way: rather than saving time, it costs time (even very small micro seconds), it's less efficient, we make more mistakes, and over time it can be energy sapping and make us far less productive as well as contributing to feeling even more overwhelmed. So much for 'multitasking' then. Multitasking appears in fact to be a myth and rushing around doing so many things thinking we are being very efficient actually impacts our thought processes and ability to be productive and efficient. However, at the same time rushing around *feels* good and *feels* as if we are getting things done so it can be hard to break free of this habit and even more so when we are surrounded by others who are also rushing around responding and reacting in the same way.

So this is why the ability to focus is the number one key skill today. The types of things that can distract us include irrelevant information, external distractions, interruptions, email, social media and a wandering mind. All of these things happen lots of times each and every day.

Digital engagement comes at a cost in face time with real people – the medium where we learn to 'read' nonverbal communication – more on this in Chapter 5 – *Face-to-Face Communication*. We may be adept and efficient at the keyboard, but we are not as proficient when it comes to reading behaviour face-to-face, in real time – particularly in sensing something emotional. Most people's emotional response can be 'read' within seconds of an interaction and if we paid close enough attention we'd catch this. According to Daniel Pink's book *A Whole New Mind*, we need to become better at reading people's faces and body language and that means paying far closer attention to people we are interacting with than we normally do. This is because facial expressions that demonstrate real feelings underneath, which are not being voiced, are visible only for a few seconds but long enough to recognise easily if you are paying attention and not distracted by your own thoughts. Remember the basic emotional responses to things discussed in Chapter 1? That's what these initial facial expressions tell you: anger, happiness, surprise, sadness, disgust and fear. They are fleeting, though, so being able to 'read' these give you vital cues and understanding but also requires very close attention on your part.

If we can fine-tune our ability to focus and pay attention when it matters, our communication skills will be much stronger and more effective.

Two core skills that help manage distraction and increase your productivity and performance levels

1) **Listening** – when we really listen we are far more in tune with the actual messages we're receiving and far less likely to misinterpret or jump to conclusions, plus we will have control of the core skill that underpins all successful human relationships. Really listening and focusing on another person requires effort but is the greatest gift we can give someone because it taps into the basic human need to feel valued and fully acknowledged. We are also far more likely to better understand any situation when we truly listen.

   How to develop listening skills: Next time you are having a conversation give it your complete focus. Override the urge to come in with your own thoughts or advice. Instead, ask questions, shut out any distractions and give the other person the gift of your attention. There are more ideas on active listening tips in Chapter 5 – *Face-to-Face Communication*.

2) **Focusing** – Once we are more aware of how to really focus and can let go of the myth of multitasking we will see a dramatic rise in our productivity levels. We will get so much more done as a result because our brain won't be in permanent 'reaction' mode, burning up the very fuel we need to stay on task.

   How to develop focusing skills: We cover this in a lot of detail in Chapter 3 – *Working Smarter*. As a start, you can become more aware of the typical sorts of distractions that are around you at any time. This may work best next time you have put some time aside for a specific project. Are you aware of how much you allow yourself to become distracted or even interrupt yourself with random thoughts, checking social media or switching to another task? It's the small tasks, especially, that can distract us most sometimes.

   Performance and excellence are additional benefits you may experience as a result of listening and focusing more – being excellent happens through focus and being able to tap into our 'flow' state – this is when we experience a state of heightened awareness, which allows us to perform at peak levels. In flow, the emotions are not just contained and channelled, but positive, energised and aligned with the task at hand. Flow states are periods of the greatest productivity and efficiency and can only happen when we are fully present and paying full attention.

   In positive psychology, flow, also known as 'the zone', is the mental state of operation in which a person performing an activity is fully immersed in a feeling of energised focus, full involvement, and enjoyment in the process of the activity. In essence, flow is characterised by complete absorption in what you are doing. Think of times when you have been involved with playing sports or a musical instrument. Or imagine for a moment that you are running a race. Your attention is focused on the movements of your body, the power of your muscles, the force of your lungs, and the feel of the street beneath your feet. You are living in the moment, utterly absorbed in the present activity. Time seems to fall away. You are tired, but you barely notice.

How to develop performance and excellence: Although many may argue that performance and excellence can be achieved mainly through hard work and effort it is actually when you are in flow that you are truly tapping into the maximum of your potential and your ability and are at the peak of your focus. The flow state has been described by the world's greatest thinkers as the most productive and creative state of mind in which to work. You can increase your ability to practise flow through mindfulness in everyday activities and bringing yourself fully into the present whenever you feel yourself beginning to or wanting to wander.

Try this

Follow these suggestions to experiment further with finding flow:

Step 1: Find a challenge. Choose something that you enjoy doing. It can be anything, whether it's playing the piano, working on some writing, skiing, horseback riding, playing golf, and so on.

Step 2: Develop your skills in order to be able to meet the challenge. Remember that if something is too easy you'll be bored – and your mind is likely to wander so you won't achieve the flow state – and if something is too hard you'll be overwhelmed and you won't be able to achieve that subconscious competence that is necessary for the flow state.

Step 3: Set clear goals. Try to be really clear on what you want to achieve and how you'll know whether you're succeeding.

Step 4: Focus completely on the task at hand. Eliminate all other distractions. You don't want anything to take your attention away from the task that you're performing; if your concentration is broken you will have to exit the state of flow.

Step 5: Make sure that you've set aside sufficient time. It is likely to take at least 15 minutes to start to get into the flow state, and a while longer after that until you're fully immersed. Once you enter the flow state you want to make sure that you make the most of it, instead of having to stop prematurely because you have to do something else.

Step 6: Monitor your emotional state. If you meet all of the requirements above, but you're having trouble entering the flow state, monitor your emotional state. If you're in an aroused state – angry, anxious, worried, and so on – try doing something that will calm you down. Do you feel that your energy level is low and you're feeling sluggish? Do something to pick up your energy levels, whether it's doing jumping jacks, having a healthy snack, reading something motivational, or calling a friend who makes you laugh.

The discipline of focus

The skill and discipline to focus is becoming a commodity in our modern world and we, myself included, undermine this skill each and every day, perhaps without even realising it. Technology and smartphones mean that we have become voracious multitaskers – perhaps texting or messaging while on our way somewhere, catching up on email and messages during lectures or when we are meant to be studying in the library or working on a project, checking what our friends are doing, 'sharing' experiences on social media even as we are experiencing them in real time, researching and studying while watching favourite TV shows on catch-up.

Part of the problem is that we can access whatever we want to on tablets and phones through live streaming and whenever we want to through catch-up TV and features like 'live pause'. There simply is no 'off' button to all the information coming in and the choices that we have. So we need to find our own ways of creating 'off' buttons.

Thinking point

Our smartphones have become Swiss army knife-like appliances that include a dictionary, calculator, web browser, email, video games, appointment calendar, voice recorder, guitar tuner, weather forecaster, satellite navigation, texter, tweeter, social media updater and flashlight. They're more powerful and do more things than the most advanced computer at IBM corporate headquarters 30 years ago. And we use them all the time, part of a 21st-century mania for cramming everything we do into every single spare moment of downtime.

Technology has given us the ability to do anything we feel like at any time – every time we respond to our phone, look up something on the internet, check email or instant messages, send a text; every single time this tweaks the novelty-seeking, reward-seeking centres of our brain, giving an enormous hit of dopamine, effectively rewarding the brain for losing focus and constantly searching for external stimulation. Our brains are not wired to multitask when we do several things at once – all that is really happening is that we are just switching from one thing to another really quickly. And every time we switch there is a cognitive cost. Yet, because of the power of dopamine, the urge to check and respond to messages or quickly look something up is in fact compelling. Why?

Dopamine is seen as crucial to learning. When the brain is presented with an unexpected reward, dopamine increases, prompting the limbic reward system to take note and remember how to repeat such a positive experience. This impacts memory and habit formation. So every time we get that hit of dopamine when we respond to our distractions, we are in effect teaching our brain to continue to do so which is why it feels so compelling to check each time we are aware of a new message or piece of information. This has a big impact on our ability to manage time efficiently.

Try this

Next time you have a bit of downtime on your hands – maybe you are waiting for someone or sitting down waiting for a train or simply eating your lunch – notice how quickly you will want to check your phone for something and be aware of the strength of that urge. Try overriding it and just doing nothing!

Our brains certainly do have the ability to process all the information we take in every day but this comes at a cost: the main problem here is that we can have trouble separating the trivial from the important and so all this information processing simply makes our brains tired because the brain perceives all of it as all having the same importance. The neurons in our brain are living cells with a metabolism: they need oxygen and glucose to survive and when they've been working hard, we experience fatigue. Everything starts to become or seem equally important. We actually need to learn how to prioritise and manage our exposure to all of this information to avoid this fatigue and consequent inattention and inability to focus.

Basic attention, the cognitive 'muscle' that lets us follow a story, see a task through to the end, learn or create, is fast becoming a precious commodity.

The research picture

Donald Broadbent is recognised as being one of the major contributors to the information processing approach. He proposed an early selection view of attention, meaning that humans process information with limited capacity and select information to be processed early (Broadbent, 1958). As psychological research has advanced, more sophisticated measures indicate that we do have an attentional filter, though it is integrated into a broader cognitive system. Mental effort is used while engaging in performing any mental task, and the greater the complexity, the greater the effort needed to solve a task. Daniel Kahneman believes there are three basic conditions which need to be met for proper completion of a task. By combining total attentional capacity, momentary mental effort and appropriate allocation policy of the attentional capacity, a person will exert enough mental effort to overcome mental tasks (in Friedenberg and Silverman, 2012). The key component is allocating enough attention, as a resource, to the task at hand. Because we now tend to switch from one task to another so rapidly, we run the risk of not allocating sufficient resources to achieve the mental effort required.

Remember the start/stop/start process means that we are not saving time. In fact, what is happening is that we are allowing ourselves to become so distracted by switching tasks that we are less efficient and less effective as a result. Every status update we read, every text message or instant message from a friend, is competing for resources in our brain with important things like what preparation we need to put in to get that report written, an essential work meeting coming up or even how best to reconcile with a close friend we've just had an argument with.

Self-check

What is going on around you right now as you read this text? Where are you sitting and what distractions are there? Is your phone within easy reach? Are you near to other digital devices? What sort of information is coming at you? When was the last time you checked your phone for messages? What do you hear? What thoughts are going through your mind?
Simply beginning to be aware of these is the first step towards overcoming distractions more effectively.

List some of the things you could do to minimise these distractions:

_____

_____

_____

_____

_____

_____

Try this small test to experience what effect multitasking has on our mental processing abilities:

(a) Draw two horizontal lines on a piece of paper
(b) Now time yourself as you carry out the two tasks that follow:
(c) On the first line, write:
◦ I am a great multitasker
(d) On the second line: write out the numbers 1–20 sequentially, like those below:

◦ 1 2 3 4 5 6 7 8 9 10 11 12 13 14 15 16 17 18 19 20
How much time did it take to do the two tasks? (Usually it's about 20 seconds.)

Now, let's multitask
Draw two more horizontal lines. This time, and again have someone time you, write a letter on one line, and then a number on the line below, then the next letter in the sentence 'I am a great multitasker' on the upper line, and then the next number in the sequence, changing from line to line. In other words, you write the letter 'I' and then the number '1' and then the letter 'a' and then the number '2' and so on, until you complete both lines.

I a.....
1 2.....

Was your time double or more what it was on the first round? You also may have made some errors and were probably frustrated since you had to 'rethink' what the next letter would be and then the next number.

Multitasking is 'switch tasking' and it actually takes up more time. If we can grasp and accept this, we are well on the way to becoming more productive and to overcoming distraction.

That brief example showed switch tasking based on something very simple, but the same process is exactly what happens when we attempt to do many things (often more complex) at the same time.

Exercise

Next time you think you are multitasking, why not stop and be aware that you are really switch tasking. Then give yourself a time limit (10 minutes or even

45 minutes) and focus on just one task and see if you can complete it better, faster, and with less energy. *Note that you may feel a compulsion to multitask because you are so conditioned to reaching for your smartphone or reacting to distraction so it may be challenging at first.*

Now, if multitasking causes so much inefficiency, what about distractions? According to the Laboratory of Neuro Imaging at the University of Southern California the average person has 70,000 thoughts per day so we are already very good at distracting ourselves without any outside help. But every distraction chips away at the amount of glucose flowing to the brain, depleting the energy it uses to do its best work on the tasks that really matter. Hence the important link between focus and productivity and performance.

Most people feel under immense pressure to be productive and to do more, which is partly why we tend to multitask so much.

However, working long hours and multitasking the whole time does not amount to being more productive. Studies show that just one hour of focused time equals four of time spent trying to finish a task while you're distracted. This is quite phenomenal when you think about it. It means planning our time and our days carefully and prioritising what is most important before we start. In other words, if your brain is most active and alert when you first wake up then it makes sense to use the first part of your day on 'brain-intensive' work such as writing, researching, dealing with a complex problem or even scheduling a challenging meeting. Most of us, though, on first waking don't even stop to have breakfast before we start checking messages, social media and email. The result is giving our brain a massive inflow of information and tasks which in effect use up the energy we needed for the important work. If we could train ourselves from the compulsion to interact with our smartphones from the minute we wake up and instead use that time for more focused work, we might notice a step-jump in productivity levels and a different way of managing our time.

Try this

1. Collect a list of all your tasks	Pull together everything you could possibly consider getting done in a day. Don't worry about the order, or the number of items up front.
2. Identify urgent vs. important	The next step is to see if you have any tasks that need immediate attention. This is work that, if not completed by the end of the day or in the next several hours, will have serious negative consequences (missed deadline etc.). Check to see if there are any high-priority dependencies that rely on you finishing up a piece of work now.
3. Assess value	Next, look at your important work and identify what carries the highest value for you. As a general practice, try to recognise exactly which types of task have top priority over the others. For example, focus on: projects with deadlines before responding to messages; setting up the new computer before re-configuring the database. Another way to assess value is to look at how many people are impacted by your work. In general, the more people involved or impacted, the higher the stakes.

4. Order tasks by estimated effort	If you have tasks that seem to tie for priority standing, check their estimates, and start on whichever one you think will take the most effort to complete. Productivity experts suggest the tactic of starting the lengthier task first. But, if you feel like you can't focus on your meatier projects before you finish up the shorter task, then go with your gut and do that. It can be motivating to check a small task off the list before diving into deeper waters.
5. Be flexible and adaptable	Uncertainty and change is a given. Know that your priorities will change, and often when you least expect them to. But – and here's the trick – you also want to stay focused on the tasks you're committed to completing.
6. Know when to cut	You probably can't get to everything on your list. After you prioritise your tasks and look at your estimates, cut the remaining tasks from your list, and focus on the priorities that you know you must and can complete for the day. Then take a deep breath, dive in and be ready for anything.

It's clear that prioritising is critical, and Dr David Rock, who has done much pioneering work in the field of neuroscience, offers some time management strategies for prioritising more effectively and insists that it must be the first thing you do before you tackle anything else when you start your day. He believes that the task of prioritising is one of the brain's most demanding processes.

Here are David Rock's time management tips:

1) Prioritise prioritising, as it's an energy-intensive activity.
2) Save mental energy for prioritising by avoiding other high-energy consuming activities such as dealing with emails.
3) Use the brain to interact with information rather than trying to store information, by creating visuals for complex ideas.
4) List projects for the day. It allows your brain to focus on comparing the elements of each project instead of using energy to hold each one in your mind.
5) Schedule the most attention-rich tasks when you have a fresh and alert mind. Making a tough decision might take 30 seconds when you are fresh, and be impossible when you're not.
6) Be aware of your own mental energy needs and schedule accordingly. Schedule blocks of time for different modes of thinking. Divide your day into blocks of time for deep thinking, having meetings, and routine tasks like responding to emails or other messages. Use this strategy to shift around the type of work you do to let your brain recover.
7) Don't think when you don't have to. To be more effective and get more done, discipline yourself to not pay attention to non-urgent tasks unless it's truly essential that you do. Learn to say no to tasks that are not among your priorities. (*adapted from "Your Brain at Work: Strategies for Overcoming Distraction, Regaining Focus and Working Smarter All Day Long", Dr David Rock, Harper Business, 2009*)

Our brains really are amazing but while the brain can seem almost boundless in its potential, it has limitations, such as processing speed, attentional limitations, working memory limitations, and sensitivity to interference, which can be both internal and external.

Your working memory

Psychologists use the term 'working memory' to describe the ability we have to hold in mind and mentally manipulate information over short periods of time. Working memory is often thought of as a mental workspace that we can use to store important information in the course of our mental activities.

Your working memory is important because it is critical to your ability to control your attention and concentrate despite distractions, learn *and* comprehend and take in what you read and generally improve your overall performance on measures of intelligence! It also improves with age. However, your working memory ability is limited.

Here are some of the situations that often lead to the loss of information from working memory.

Distraction. An unrelated thought springing to mind, or an interruption such as a telephone ringing or someone speaking to us, can be sufficient to divert attention so that the working memory contents are rapidly lost.

Trying to hold in mind too much information. There is a limit to how much information can be held in working memory. For example, most of us would not be successful in attempting to multiply the numbers 739 and 891 in our heads, simply because the amount of information that has to be stored in the course of this calculation exceeds the capacity of most people's working memory.

Engaging in a demanding task. Activities that require difficult mental processing reduce the amount of space in working memory to store information. This can result in a loss of other information that is already held.

If we know and understand the limitations of our working memory we will become better at controlling our attention, and managing distractions and our ability to concentrate and focus when we need to.

So what is the best way to go about training the brain to channel energy in an efficient and effective manner so you can accomplish more in less time? One way to accomplish more is simply to slow down. This may feel counter-intuitive but is very effective.

Try this

1) **'Routinise' your day**
   When something is routine, it can help to diminish stress and minimises the amount of decisions you have to make each day which use up brain energy. Look at all the tasks that you do in a day. Which are the ones that you could turn into easy-to-manage routines? Doing this lessens the toll on your brain for making decisions and this brain energy can be used for other tasks that do require more focus. Building routines into the day can be relatively minor-seeming tasks like putting clothes out ready for the next morning the night before, packing your bag or case the evening before with

key documents you need for the day ahead or having everything to hand to create a nutritious breakfast so that these things become automated during busy working days.

2) **Know when a task requires undivided attention**
Switching brain channels (focus) repeatedly actually reduces your memory recall. Think of your brain as a computer. If you are working within multiple programmes and have numerous windows open on your screen so you can quickly jump from programme to programme, you may find that your computer has a higher tendency of locking up. That is, when you have 15 windows open at once on your computer, and you attempt to pull up that report you're working on, it's not uncommon for your computer to run slowly or to totally freeze up, often causing you to lose all the data since your last 'save'.

   The exact same thing happens in your brain. When you're trying to perform multiple tasks, each of which probably requires your undivided attention, your brain gets overloaded, as it can only process information from one channel at a time. Therefore, it makes sense that if an assignment or project requires your full attention you focus only on that one task. Once that task is complete, then you can go back to doing the other tasks you normally do. This step will save you lots of rework, as you're more prone to making mistakes when your brain is overloaded.

3) **Use a tool to help you**
To avoid taxing your brain, write down items you can refer to quickly. For example, if you have a list of items you need to refer to often (such as numerical information or keyboard shortcuts) put the list next to your phone or computer for quick access. This is a simple thing to do and stops you wasting precious brain energy on mundane information.

4) **Allow your mind to reboot**
If you are busy on a number of high-energy tasks allow your mind to reboot. The human brain uses more energy than any other part of the body. As such, it needs constant replenishment. Rest is one of the key components to increasing personal energy and productivity. So every two to three hours, stop what you are doing and allow yourself to do something completely different for 15 to 20 minutes. At the end of this rest period, you are more likely to feel refreshed, alert, and ready to tackle more – and, even better, do so with fewer mistakes than if you ploughed through your tasks without this reboot period. However, it does require conscious effort and a decision and desire to do this. Remember that it is going to be far more tempting and compelling to *not* take breaks and to just keep going, even more so when the pressure is on.

5) **Take a brain break**
Most workplaces will have a lunch break and two 15-minute breaks throughout the day. Do you ever allow yourself these sorts of breaks? Most people do not, and as such, they're not giving their mind a true break from the stresses of the day. Use your break time to walk around or go outside into your garden if you have one, sit outside, or just close your eyes and meditate. Do whatever you like during these 15 minutes to clear your head and give your brain a rest. If you really can't afford a 15-minute break in your day, then turn off your mind as you walk somewhere to get something. Give your mind a short burst of total break from workday tasks. To function at peak levels on a consistent basis, regular breaks are essential.

6) **Do more with less stress**
Multitasking is a part of our world even if we are not good at it. If you want to succeed, you need to learn how to organise work and information so it doesn't overwhelm you and cause unnecessary stress. By simply slowing down and working up to the performance level you need and want, you can work effectively and increase productivity. It is about tapping into your highest mental abilities to function.

Managing distraction is a vital part of conserving brain energy and achieving higher performance levels.

When we take a closer look at the brain's sensitivity to distractions this can be loosely grouped into what is termed external interference and internal interference. Remember the communications process model in the last chapter. These are also the sorts of things that are part of 'noise' and impact how well we interpret or receive a message.

External interferences can be irrelevant distractions such as the noise around us in a restaurant while we are trying to have a business or personal conversation. External interference is also linked to multitasking, which we now know the brain is extremely sensitive to.

Self-check

Can you recall when you last experienced being distracted by noise, perhaps in a restaurant, or by multitasking? Or when it might be likely to happen in the future? You can probably come up with an example either in the very recent past or in the very near future.

Internal interferences happen inside our heads while we are already engaged in a task or conversation. Mind wandering can happen when we are actually focused on something and yet our mind wanders away to something that is totally irrelevant to the task we are focusing on. This may be something we feel anxious about and is very likely to be something that is not linked to the present moment at all but rather focused on the past or the future. Mind wandering can happen seemingly without our control, which is why it is so important to tame the wandering mind and bring it back into the present moment.

When did this last happen to you? Again, it may have been very recently. Mind wandering is just what the brain tends to do. Have you ever tried using mindfulness to help yourself be more centred and engaged?

Try this

Quick mindfulness exercise:

You can try being mindful right here and right now. Start by becoming more aware of your breathing (try taking some nice, deep, slow breaths), your posture, your body, the noises you can hear around you, what you can see. Do this while at the same time letting go of any thoughts and distractions that come in. Doing this practice just five minutes a day can really help.

Internal multitasking occurs when we have an external goal or focus but are engaged with an internal goal at the same time. For instance, listening to someone speaking or reading this text while thinking about something else at the same time, like planning what is for lunch or dinner or worrying about something that we will be doing in the future or about something that has already happened.

We do this so often without even realising it or the impact it may have. This is why practising mindfulness is so key to helping us learn to focus and be present.

Let's revisit the communication model from Chapter 1 and the 'noise' component. Noise is any type of disruption that interferes with the transmission or interpretation of information from the sender to the receiver. Active listening, which requires focus, and making use of mindfulness to help us focus are both key to successful encoding and decoding of messages (how you choose to communicate and how you choose to interpret if you are on the receiving end of communication) as well as overcoming all the 'noise'.

We are constantly exposed to noise, and this only seems to be increasing. This noise includes email, notifications, text messages, phone calls, other people, website pop ups, browser tabs, videos, and many other factors. Revisiting the communication process model we can see that the kinds of 'noise' which can interfere with our attention and our communication message have probably increased due to the amount of information overload and distractions we have around us.

Transmission phase

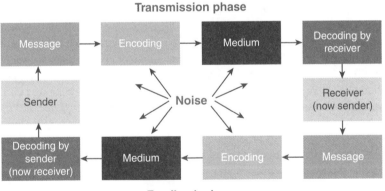

Feedback phase

Over time, people have changed their expectations on how responsive they are to these kinds of distractions. For example, it has become perfectly acceptable to be on holiday or at the theatre or be engaged in a conversation, to suddenly hear a text message or email notification and actually respond to it there and then. The ability to instantly check messages and respond creates a new kind of demand and an expectation of *having* to respond immediately. This has set a new standard for how we 'should' interact with technology. This in turn creates a never-ending impression of urgency in our brains so that all of these types of distractions become equally important to respond to as quickly as possible.

None of this is helped by the fact that our brains very much like and enjoy responding in this way because doing so triggers production of dopamine neurotransmitters (pleasure chemicals) in the brain, which can become very addictive.

The ability to focus is a hard-won skill – yet entirely within our power to win. We can function perfectly well in our distraction-filled environments and indeed do so, but at an increasing cost to our productivity, ability to focus and our stress levels. This is only worsening. The more we can increase our awareness of the need to focus and pay attention and adopt strategies that help us to do that, the better we will become at processing and interpreting information and messages more accurately. We need to learn how to control our noisy environment so that we can function effectively within it and enjoy the many advantages and positives that all this technology and accessibility provide us with.

We have cognitive control. We process the world around us through attention, so it is our ability to control this that is so vital when it comes to communication and interacting with others.

What we can do to handle distraction

We can change our behaviour by *setting and following specific rules*. We can also change our brain by *cognitive training*.

Establish rules. When we are doing something that demands high-quality work and especially when it is time sensitive, shut down email, turn off the smartphone, shut the door, and remove all possible sources of distraction. To be productive with important tasks, we need to give high-quality singular attention to what we are doing. Performance quality decreases if we allow frequent interruptions. We should practise the skill of concentration by turning off all distractions and committing our attention to a single task. The best way is to start small, maybe five minutes per day, and work up to larger chunks of time. If we find our mind wandering, just return to the task at hand. It's just like getting fit – we have to build the 'muscle' to be focused.

We can use multitasking productively with boring, easier and less critical tasks. However, it is important to choose tasks carefully to make sure that they can be done while multitasking. This requires honesty and discipline. The main problem with multitasking is that we focus on doing several tasks that actually require different types of brain energy.

The secret is to work on related tasks together. That stops your brain from having to pause when you move to something new. Think about it – if you're in the middle of creating a presentation and then stop to make a phone call, that's when you'll find your ability to focus on the presentation when you come back to it is far less. In contrast, if you are reading related information and making notes, then you are more likely to be efficient. It's the same principle people use when cooking a meal, where several related tasks are on the go at the same time.

Some people use caffeine or other stimulants to improve their performance. Most of these are not really ideal for the purpose of improving attention and memory but are used to help improve cognitive abilities. Some of the effects include increased arousal, concentration, working memory and other cognitive functions. However, intake of these can actually lead to decreased performance in the long term due to side effects and changes in the brain.

Putting it into practice

1) Start paying attention to your own behaviours

Try this self-assessment test:

- Take note of how you use media in different settings including home, work and in social situations.
- Ask yourself how you feel when multitasking. Do you feel in control or do you feel overwhelmed? Can you pinpoint how this feels?
- How does multitasking affect your performance, mood or level of stress?
- Set an alarm to remind yourself of your behaviour. Just pause and pay attention to your behaviour and what you are doing. This can be as simple as getting used to observing yourself reaching for your phone and how often you do it. Doing this raises your awareness and you may start to do it less now that you understand the impact this has on your abilities to function well. Self-awareness is one of the keys to self-control.

2) Challenge yourself

- Just because you are surrounded by demands and expectations for multitasking does not mean that you have to feel out of control.
- Exercise your cognitive control by learning how to better interact with your environment based on your goals.
- Challenge your routines. For example, stop texting or messaging while you are doing something else. Have digital free periods throughout the day.
- Avoid distraction when you are engaged in important tasks. That means taking necessary steps to put distraction out of the way.
- Practise single tasking for an extended period of time. Do one thing at a time.
- Retreat to nature for short periods in your day.

3) Become more self-aware

- Keep learning more about how your brain works. Then look for points when you can relate this to how you spend your time, how you respond to things and how to interact with others.
- Keep trying out different approaches that make sense for you.

4) Try being mindful

- Mindfulness is on the increase – just 5–10 minutes a day can increase your ability to be present and in the moment and can train your brain to be more focused.

5) Write more

- Write things down, keep lists – when you have a lot of tasks to accomplish (and who doesn't?) get them out of your head and onto paper.
- Consider keeping a journal to jot down how you are using your time. Most of us charge through our day going from one thing to the next and then wonder why we feel so tired or why we fail to get things done. Slotting in reflection time to write and plan at the beginning and end of your day can increase productivity significantly.
- We have far more control over our ability to focus than we may at first think. We can all learn to interact with our environment in a more effective way that benefits how we work and how we communicate.

Our understanding of how our brains interact with our environment might guide our decision-making ability and allow us to make more informed decisions, thereby increasing the health and the qualities of our lives and relationships.

So what? How you can use the information in this chapter to overcome distraction

This chapter has focused on giving you some insight into the importance of managing distractions and the huge impact that doing this will have both on your productivity levels (more on this in Chapter 3 too!) and on your communication skills.

Understanding how distractions impact our brains and our behaviour and knowing what we do about our amazing brains from Chapter 1, you should be able to identify ways that you can hone your ability to focus and be more in the moment. Doing this will enable you to 'read' emotional cues with agility as well as tap into your active listening skills when you need to. This 'when you need to' approach is also important because focusing our attention in this way requires consistent effort and it isn't going to be possible to sustain this level of effort all the time. That's why trying some of the ideas out in 'low-stake' situations such as interactions with friends and monitoring your use of your phone and social media is helpful because you will notice an immediate impact, which in turn you will be able to transfer to higher-stake situations such as job interviews or situations where there just may be more at stake.

Further reading

Ekman, Paul. 2007. *Emotions Revealed, Second Edition: Recognizing Faces and Feelings to Improve Communication and Emotional Life*. Holt.

Huffington, Arianna. 2015. *Thrive: The Third Metric to Redefining Success and Creating a Happier Life*. W. H. Allen.

Huffington, Arianna. 2016. *The Sleep Revolution: Transforming Your Life, One Night at a Time*. W. H. Allen.

Pink, Daniel. 2011. *A Whole New Mind: Why Right-Brainers Will Rule the Future*. Marshall Cavendish.

Rock, Daniel, 2009. *Your Brain at Work: Strategies for Overcoming Distraction, Regaining Focus and Working Smarter All Day Long*, Harper Business.

Williams, Mark & Penman, Danny. 2011. *Mindfulness: A Practical Guide to Finding Peace in a Frantic World*. Piatkus.

Working Smarter

What's in this chapter:

- Did you know? Facts and statistics about working smarter
- Why your brain needs fuel to work smart
- Bringing productivity into a typical day
- The role of willpower and mindset
- How to deal with stress
- Dealing with procrastination
- So what? How you can use the information in this chapter to boost your skills

---

Did you know?

Facts and statistics about working smarter

- If you want to work smart, you have to be smart. If you want to create value, your brain 'muscle' must be as strong as possible. You have to constantly train your brain muscle and challenge it to new levels; both the analytical and the creative part of your brain are very important.
- If you want to work smart, you need to be in good health, regularly taking care of your body with exercise and diet.
- 20% of the most important tasks lead to 80% of progress so it makes sense to focus on that 20%. This is the well-known Pareto principle.
- A 2011 study published in the *Sleep* journal and supported by the National Sleep Foundation and Centers for Disease Control and Prevention found that sleep deprivation costs American companies billions of dollars a year in lost productivity (Kessler et al., 2011).

Productivity is a measure of how much you accomplish and comes from working smart, not how busy you are. So it's far better to learn how to work intelligently, and to use leverage to achieve more with your time and resources. This will increase your productivity – and help you find extra time to do other things.

You may have come across a lot of discussion about working smarter. The key to greater productivity is to work smarter, not harder, yet sometimes it is hard to distinguish between the two. Ask anyone writing a report, or think about when you are working to a deadline. The temptation will always be to put in long hours, sometimes working until late into the night. Yet, understanding that our brain's energy gets used up much faster this way with a diminished result at the end, you may decide to work in a different way. Working smarter simply means *choosing* to work differently so that you have more energy and are more productive and get more done while at the same time achieving a healthy balance.

Working smarter boosts productivity and creativity, and saves precious energy for the things that really matter. In fact, much of working smarter is also related to managing our distractions and learning how to focus as outlined in Chapter 2 – *How to Overcome Distraction*. But how do you know that what you're achieving is the absolute best it can be? The answer is, you don't. Working smarter, though, gives you more focus and an improved ability to focus on the finer detail of a task. You get more time to be aware of and to notice details that, when taken care of, can create something superior. This, in turn, makes you more valuable in the workplace, makes it easier to tap into your skills and potential and will make you enjoy your job/work/tasks more, because you know you're producing to the best of your capabilities.

Working very hard can be an easy habit to slip into. Sometimes it's difficult to switch off at the end of the day or take time out in the evenings or on the weekend and to stop thinking about work or deadlines. Sometimes it is just far easier and even feels better to keep going – after all, the natural compulsion if you are working hard on a deadline or project is to keep piling the work on for longer and longer. And even if you are not working on something specific you may still feel compelled to 'keep on top' of emails or tasks and fall into the habit of just never taking a break. It's also become a type of 'badge of honour' to be busy.

We need to understand far better how to use our mental resources more effectively and how to increase optimum performance and thinking. The brain has a major part to play here and understanding better some of the links between our brain's energy and how we use it is key. Do you find yourself creative, focused and speeding ahead in the morning and then by late afternoon perhaps feeling sluggish, making mistakes and flitting from one thing to the next? It could be your brain has simply run out of working capacity. The conscious, thinking, analytical part of your brain sits immediately behind your forehead and we all totally over-estimate the capacity of this part of the brain to concentrate and work for an extended amount of time. The processing power of this part of our brain is something like 2,000 pieces of information per second; this in itself is amazing, but its capacity is quite limited in terms of the amount of time it can effectively do that for. So if you are spending the first part of your day checking emails and messages this is actually using up valuable energy that you might need to conserve for tasks where you really do need the best bits of your brain and your thinking. Yet most of us will instead check our emails and messages at the beginning of the day and genuinely feel this is important and a worthwhile use of time. One helpful habit to adopt may be to not do this at all until you have worked for at least two hours and see what happens!

Why your brain needs fuel to work smart

Your brain uses glucose as a kind of 'fuel'. Our brain needs a steady supply of energy, but it can only get this from a type of sugar called glucose. Glucose keeps our brains awake and alert. So at all times, we have a certain glucose level in our blood. The most important part here is that we are actually in full control of how we release glucose to our blood and our brains.

Not surprisingly glucose is linked to what we eat. You can feed your brain and knowing how to do this and what foods to eat can make an immediate impact. The glucose your brain needs comes from the carbohydrates you eat, but only certain kinds. These include wholemeal bread, pasta, porridge and pulses, which take time for your body to break down and so release their glucose slowly and steadily. Chocolate, biscuits and other sugary snacks are, sadly, not so good for your brain. They release their sugar so quickly that your brain will peak but then quickly crash afterwards leaving you feeling less energised than before. So, part of working smarter has to be about looking after our brains, knowing what foods benefit the brain and understanding better how to use that energy.

Foods that boost your brain's energy

Take a look at the list below and try to identify how often you include these foods in your day-to-day diet.

Which types of food?	How do they benefit your brain?
Omega 3 fats are found in oily fish like salmon and trout as well as in pumpkin seeds, linseed, walnuts, chia seeds and soya beans.	Omega 3 fats have essential fatty acids (EFAs) which cannot be made by the body so they need to come from your diet or supplements. These fats help with managing stress and aiding good memory as well as helping to make the feel-good brain chemical serotonin. Pumpkin seeds also have zinc which is vital for enhancing thinking and memory skills. The magnesium in them also gives a welcome happiness boost.
Blueberries	Great for improving memory function and well known as a 'super food'.
B vitamins – B6, B12 and folic acid – chicken, fish, eggs and leafy greens	The B vitamins boost your general vitality and energy levels.
Broccoli	Broccoli is great source of vitamin K, which is known to enhance cognitive function and improve brainpower.
Bee pollen	The wide range of nutrients found in bee pollen makes it a great natural energiser. Pollens are about 40% protein and are rich in folic acid, free amino acids, and lots of B-complex, which can help keep you

	going all day by enhancing the brain's stamina and fighting off fatigue. So, forget the cup of coffee. Add a teaspoon of bee pollen to a smoothie or shake for a boost of energy when you need it for those early morning meetings or that extra push in the early afternoon.
Dark chocolate	Now this has to be chocolate that is very high in cacao so make sure you buy high-quality organic dark chocolate. Chocolate improves cognitive function and is also one of the most powerful antioxidants in the world – it's got 15 times more antioxidants than blueberries and 20 times more than green tea.
Spinach	Popeye was right! Nitrates can be found in spinach, increasing blood flow to the brain and improving mental performance.

Try this

- Looking at the above list, think of easy ways you can introduce some of these foods into your diet.
- Try charting what you eat for a day – how much of your diet includes the foods above? Are you eating more sugar than is good for you?
- Think of a demanding day ahead or a period when you perhaps need to study and work intensively. Plan what you will eat that day or during that time period around the brain food suggestions above.

Bringing productivity into a typical day

The other part of working smart is about how we organise our day and our time.

Different people work in different ways but most ways of working place value on the ability to pay attention, concentrate and focus. People who take a break, sit back and think or take an afternoon nap might be perceived as unproductive or lazy, especially in the workplace. Companies like Google that provide things like 'nap pods' might be thought of as quirky, but could it be these companies understand the brain better than most?

Take these two examples of very different work habits and let's look at them through the lens of productivity and working smarter. As you're reading this think also about how you typically spend your day and your time.

Rachel works for 10 hours pretty much without stopping; she is at her desk, head down most of the day, when she isn't running to and from meetings, and she eats lunch at her desk. She begins work at about 80% of her capacity, instinctively pacing herself because she knows she's got a long day ahead. By lunchtime she's dropped to 60% of her capacity and is feeling fatigued. After 4pm she's averaging about 40% capacity. As a result, her thinking is uncreative, she makes errors and has to go over her work again to correct them and her enjoyment of the work is low. By the end of the day she feels exhausted and has little energy to think about doing things outside of work in her leisure time. As a result she may well come home, eat a ready meal and then slump in front of the TV on the sofa.

James works entirely differently. He works intensely for around an hour to 90 minutes, and then takes a 15-minute break before working again. At lunchtime he goes out either for a walk, to the gym or to have lunch with friends. At around 3pm, he closes his eyes at his desk and takes a rest. Sometimes he just lets his mind wander; sometimes he has a 15–20-minute nap. Finally, between 4.30pm and 5pm, James takes a 15-minute walk outside. At the end of the day he sits back for 15 minutes and reflects on his day and makes a list of what he has learnt and what he will do tomorrow. He knows from research that people who do this increase productivity by as much as 23%. In the evening James spends time on his own interests or seeing friends.

Who would you say was the most productive? If we look at the numbers for James and Rachel it is interesting. James takes off a total of two hours during his 10 hours at work; during the remaining eight he's working at an average of 80% of his capacity, so he's delivering just under 6½ hours of work. Rachel's average work capacity over 10 hours is 60% which means she effectively delivers six hours of work. James is actually more productive than Rachel because the breaks enable him to work at 80% of his capacity. Because James is more focused and alert than Rachel, he also makes fewer mistakes, is more creative and enjoys the work. And at the end of the day he also still has energy for his own interests.

This rhythmic pattern, switching between focus and down time, between effort and renewal has been found to be the most effective way to work smart and be more productive. Psychologist K. Anders Ericsson, Professor of Psychology at Florida State University, who studies expert performers, found they do indeed work hard but also take planned rest periods. This contributes to the learning and helps skills to be embedded, making them accessible for longer and their abilities deeper. Our brain requires breaks to work productively. Most people will say that there are no more hours in a day they can work. So they need to be able to work smarter.

Counter-intuitively, doing less may well be the answer. Many innovative companies are adopting this work style. There is also evidence that levels of employee engagement are a positive by-product of the approach. People who like their job and are willing to go above and beyond their basic duties – a trait that many studies have correlated with higher performance and productivity. In 2009, Harter et al. conducted a meta-analysis encompassing 199 research studies across 152 organisations in 44 industries and 26 countries. They statistically calculated the available data on business/work unit-level relationship between employee engagement and performance outcomes within each study. The studies covered 32,394 business/work units and 955,905 employees. Their findings quantified significant differences between business units ranking in the top and bottom 25% on engagement. They found an 18% drop in productivity between the top and bottom performers. Additionally, there was a 60% drop in quality (measured by defects in products).

Self-check

Try defining how you spend a typical day at work or at study. What is your typical pattern of behaviour? What do you tend to do first thing when you wake up? What sort of prioritising of your day do you tend to do, if any? How often do you take a break? What sorts of foods do you tend to eat for breakfast? What about snacks and lunchtime? Do you ever notice your energy dipping at different times of the day?

Try this

For a week keep a record of how you are spending your time. This will immediately raise your awareness of when you are productive and when you are not and how you fill your time. Once you have done this for one week list some areas where you could build in some immediate changes. These need only be small at first but could be about building new habits such as planning your day before you check email or routinising some of your daily tasks and getting sufficient sleep when you need to. 'Routinising' can be as simple as packing what you need for the next day the night before, planning meals that you will cook and having specific times of the day when you do certain things like ordering your desk or checking your messages. This is also discussed in Chapter 2 – *How to Overcome Distraction*.

Keeping an activity log

Keeping an activity log for several days helps you to understand better how you are spending your time and when you perform at your best. Remember this is an exercise and the purpose of doing something like this is simply to get an immediate awareness of how you spend your time. The results may surprise you.

Without modifying your behaviour, note down the things you do as you do them.

Every time you change activities, whether that is working, making coffee, cooking, talking to colleagues or friends, note down the time of the change.

As well as recording activities you could boost this exercise by adding in notes about how you feel and whether you are alert, flat, tired, energetic.

TIME	Monday	Tuesday	Wednesday	Thursday	Friday	Saturday	Sunday
6.00							
7.00							
8.00							
9.00							
10.00							
11.00							
12.00							
13.00							
14.00							
15.00							
16.00							
17.00							
18.00							
19.00							
20.00							
21.00							
22.00							
23.00							
24.00							

Keeping this log, even for a short time, will immediately highlight to you how you are spending your time and energy and you should be able to identify areas where you could make some immediate changes.

The role of willpower

Willpower is an interesting part of working smarter. Again, we need to understand more about willpower and what it is. We can be extremely determined to make changes but can find it very difficult in practice. Willpower is the engine of self-control, the ability to manage thoughts, emotions and harmful habits and override momentary desires. Not much gets done without it. In a world of instant gratification, delaying something isn't a popular choice – not surprisingly, because self-regulation is hard. It's hard for brain neurons to resist an easier path. The use of willpower also burns up resources. To stay on task, resist an impulsive action, or remain disciplined expends mental energy. That has to somehow be replaced. Self-regulation expert Roy Baumeister, co-author of *Willpower: Why Self-Control is The Secret to Success*, has documented that after long hours of staying disciplined, self-regulation tends to flag at night. This explains why after a day of healthy eating it can be very difficult to resist some chocolate or one more glass of wine in the evening – I speak for myself here too!

Luckily, researchers say willpower is something we can all build like a muscle. We can improve our ability to hold off temptations at hand and persevere for a later reward.

Mental resources are depleted by self-regulating processes such as resisting temptation, restraining aggression and coping with fear. Self-control is a limited resource that must be resupplied regularly; each act of self-regulation makes it harder to perform another, because it eats up precious mental resources needed for discipline (Baumeister and Tierney, 2012).

Achievement takes effort, and effort requires command of a brain function known as 'effortful control'. Part of the executive attention function system, a disciplined effortful control mechanism is essential to self-control and the ability to resist temptation. It regulates impulse control, which prevents you from checking email when you're trying to complete a task.

Nobel prize-winning psychologist Daniel Kahneman notes that people who are simultaneously challenged by a demanding cognitive task and a temptation are more likely to yield to the temptation because it's easier than focusing on the demanding task. Similarly, people who are 'cognitively busy' are more likely to make selfish choices. He also points out that a few drinks have the same effect, as does a sleepless night – the self-control of 'morning people' is impaired at night, and vice versa.

Knowing this shows us that managing our willpower and its limitations can be very powerful. It may not be possible or realistic to do this every single day but it should be possible during periods where we need to work on a specific project and be at our absolute best.

The right mindset

Other researchers have found that self-regulation depletes energy in the brain in the form of blood glucose (Gailliot et al., 2007). Subjects given sugary drinks were able to replenish resources to take on hard tasks that demanded self-control. So there may well be times when it helps to have more sugar!

However, there is another energy source that you can tap into and that is your own belief system and the motivation that drives that. This is why self-awareness – a real understanding of yourself – is so vital. If you are able to tap into this and prepare yourself for key challenges knowing that you are, in fact, in control, this can power you through rather than being overcome by a sense of feeling overwhelmed. Mindset is a simple idea discovered by world-renowned Stanford University psychologist Carol Dweck, a leading researcher in the field of motivation through her decades of research on achievement and success – a simple idea that makes all the difference. In a fixed mindset, people believe their basic qualities, like their intelligence or talent, are simply fixed traits. In a growth mindset, people believe that their most basic abilities can be developed through dedication and hard work – brains and talent are just the starting point. This view creates a love of learning and a resilience that is essential for great accomplishment.

> Just because some people can do something with little or no training, it doesn't mean that others can't do it (and sometimes do it even better) with training.
>
> Carol Dweck, *Mindset: The New Psychology of Success* (2007)

Self-check

What sort of mindset do you have? – Go through these questions and try to answer them as spontaneously as you can:

Do you believe that you're born with a certain amount of intelligence that can't be changed?

Do you believe that intelligence can increase or decrease depending on whether or not you spend time exercising your mind?

Do you believe that you can learn new things but you can't necessarily change your underlying level of intelligence or do you believe that learning new things can actually increase your underlying intelligence?

Is talent something you're born with rather than something you can develop?

Do you think that if you practise something for long enough you can in fact develop a talent for it?

Do you believe that people with a particularly strong skill were born with a higher level of natural ability?

You may never have asked yourself these sorts of questions before and you may even be surprised by some of your beliefs.

Did you know that it's possible to grow new brain cells? This process is called 'neurogenesis' and scientists used to think it wasn't possible. However, the most recent research has found that it does actually happen (Frisén and Ernst, 2015).

> Neuroplasticity is the brain's ability to reorganise itself by forming new neural connections throughout life. Neuroplasticity allows the neurons (nerve cells) in the brain to adjust their activities in response to new situations or to changes in their environment.

One of the strongest findings in neuroplasticity is that attention and how we use attention is dramatic in its ability to physically alter the brain and enlarge functional circuits. What this means is that if we focus and give attention to a new skill or activity, especially one that might be cognitively demanding such as learning a foreign language, this is more likely to boost processing speed and expand or create functional networks in our brains. Surely this also means that we are also capable of operating far below our optimum level partly because we give up too easily? Working smarter is not a shortcut to success by any means. We still need to 'work hard' to achieve better than average results. Quite often, though, what we simply need is to keep at something for a focused period of time and in a consistent way. Most of the time it is far easier not to do that.

How to deal with stress

Many of us report feeling under stress due to increased work and financial pressures, deadlines and numerous demands on our time. And it may feel that there is not much we can do about stress. But you have more control over stress than you might think. Stress management is all about taking charge: of your lifestyle, thoughts, emotions, and the way you deal with problems. No matter how stressful your life seems, there are steps you can take to relieve the pressure and regain control.

Cortisol is a chemical in our brains that gets released when we feel under pressure, for example when we feel overwhelmed by work tasks and working too hard but at the same time not being as productive as we could be. The problem with cortisol, though, is that, like dopamine hits, it feels good. Cortisol makes us feel like we're empowered and energised and getting a high. What we are really doing, though, is wearing down our bodies. Cortisol is a natural chemical and one that we need for survival but it's actually intended for use in life-or-death situations rather than for everyday living.

We are, to quite a great extent, in control over how much cortisol we have. Normally, it's naturally present in the body at higher levels in the morning, and at its lowest at night. Although stress isn't the only reason that cortisol is secreted into the bloodstream, it has been termed 'the stress hormone' because it's also secreted in higher levels during the body's stress response and is responsible for several stress-related changes in the body. Small increases of cortisol have some positive effects including quick bursts of energy for survival reasons, heightened memory functions, a burst of increased immunity and lower sensitivity to pain.

While cortisol is an important and helpful part of the body's response to stress, it's important that the body's relaxation response is activated so the body's functions can return to normal following a stressful event. Unfortunately, in our current high-stress culture, the body's stress response is activated so often that the body doesn't always have a chance to return to normal, resulting in a state of chronic stress and constant high levels of cortisol being released into the body.

Try this

10 stressbusting techniques to try

It is really important that you are able to start to understand what contributes to your own stress and identify ways of managing this more effectively:

1. Understand where the stress is coming from

When we feel stressed it can all feel like one big mess with stress coming from every angle and with even small issues and disappointments hitting us hard. In this case we often become very defensive and blaming. This is unproductive in many ways. Instead of feeling like you're struggling day to day, identify what it is you're actually stressed about. Is it a specific project at work, an upcoming exam, a dispute with your boss, a pile of laundry, a fight with your family?

By getting specific and pinpointing the stressors in your life, you're one step closer to getting organised and taking action. You can also try labelling and reappraising – see more on this in Chapter 1 – *Your Amazing Brain*.

2. Identify what you can control

When we feel stressed we will tend to put our energy and focus onto the things we cannot control, like what someone else *might* say or do or the state of the economy. Focus instead on what you *can* control – you can control how you respond, how you accomplish work, how you spend your time and what you spend your money on as well as what you choose to focus your attention on.

The worst thing for stress is trying to take control over uncontrollable things. Because when you inevitably fail – since it's beyond your control – you only get more stressed out and feel helpless. So after you've thought through what's stressing you, identify the stressors that you can control, and determine the best ways to take action. Doing what's within your power moves you forward and is invigorating at the same time.

3. Do what you love

It's much easier to handle pockets of stress when you spend time doing things that you genuinely enjoy – this is about balance and not having all of your energy bound up in work, study and deadlines. Make time for your own interests and take plenty of healthy breaks too. This becomes easier to do once you have a better handle on how you manage your time.

4. Manage your time well

One of the biggest stressors for many people is a *perceived* lack of time. Their to-do list expands, while time flies. How often have you wished for more hours in the day or heard others lament their lack of time? But you've got more time than you think. Becoming more aware of how you are using your time will help, as will some of the smart working tips in this chapter!

5. Create a toolbox of techniques

Have strategies in place that work for you. Whether that's using deep breathing, eating healthfully, practising mindfulness or learning to identify and monitor stressors – there are a wealth of small things you can do to help manage stress.

6. Pick off the negotiables from your plate

Review your daily and weekly activities to see what you can 'pick off' your plate. Ask yourself questions like 'do [my activities] mesh with my goals and values? Am I doing things that give my life meaning? Am I doing the right amount of things?' Reducing your stack of negotiable tasks can greatly reduce your stress.

7. Are you leaving yourself especially vulnerable to stress?

Whether you perceive something as a stressor depends in part on your current state of mind and body. This can be as simple as whether you've had breakfast that day or are feeling physically fit and feeling strong. So if you're not getting sufficient sleep or physical activity during the week, you may be leaving yourself especially susceptible to stress. When you're sleep deprived, sedentary and filled to the brim with coffee, even the smallest stressors can have a huge impact!

8. Preserve good boundaries

If you're a people pleaser, saying no can feel like you're abandoning someone, have become a 'terrible person' or are just being impolite and selfish. But of course that couldn't be further from the truth. The few seconds of discomfort you may experience when you say 'no' are well worth avoiding the stress of taking on an extra activity or doing something that doesn't contribute value to your life.

One thing about productive, happy people is that they're very protective of their time and having their boundaries crossed.

9. Realise there's a difference between worrying and caring

Sometimes, our mindset can boost stress, so a small issue expands into a pile of problems. We continue worrying, somehow thinking that this is a productive – or at least inevitable – response to stress. But we mistake worry for action. Worrying is far more about attempting to control the future while caring is taking positive action. For example: fretting about your finances does nothing but get you worked up (and likely prevents you from taking action). Caring about your finances, however, means creating a budget, paying bills on time, using vouchers and reducing how often you dine out.

10. Embrace failure

Another mindset that can exacerbate stress is perfectionism. Trying to be mistake-free and essentially spending your days walking on eggshells is exhausting and anxiety provoking for yourself as well as those around you. Talk about putting pressure on yourself! And as we all know but tend to forget: perfection is actually impossible. On the other hand, if you are striving to be your best, then healthy achievement and growth mostly come from making mistakes. So get out there, take action and make mistakes and then learn from them. You'll also become more resilient in the process which puts you in a far better position to handle stress.

Dealing with procrastination

No chapter on working smarter can leave out procrastination. According to studies, 98% of us procrastinate and we are all, in fact, naturally prone to it (Steel, 2007). So working smarter will not necessarily result in never procrastinating. The trick is to understand when we do it and to reduce the frequency of it happening. It can even be possible to procrastinate productively! Since it's human nature to do it we may as well use it to our benefit.

The most common form of procrastination is grabbing our smartphones to check email, Facebook, Twitter, Pinterest or some other form of social media. It is possible to lose entire chunks of time to this and doing this does not help you make progress on anything – really it is time wasted at the expense of something much more important and remember, your poor brain does not know the difference so will treat the flood of incoming information and images as equally important as the task you are trying to accomplish. Control your use of technology and social media – decide for yourself when you will check these rather than being at the mercy of them all day long. Although this can be hard to do, the impact is immediate.

Try this

Try a digital detox! Try switching off your phone for just one day and not checking any social media at all. I promise, you will be surprised at how much more you get done. Then, try to make this a regular habit when you need blocks of time to work on something important.

Procrastinating productively, though, is something different and is about deciding what else you could get done. This could perhaps be making some notes for another project or assignment that you can use at another time or sorting out your filing system.

The best way to deal with procrastination is to break down a project into smaller parts and to take action, no matter how small. Whole books have been written on procrastination so we are not going to be able to cover everything here. Perhaps it's useful instead to have a few notes to help avoid it.

Putting it into practice

1) Always use the first 30 minutes of any task to work

This may sound familiar: you start the work day/study session by telling yourself you're 'just going to check email/Facebook/Twitter/Reddit for five minutes, then get to work'. Before you know it, five minutes has dragged into two hours, and two hours has dragged into four hours, and you realise you've spent half your day sucked into a never-ending loop of checking email, social media, YouTube, and your favourite viral news sites. I am sure you can identify with this!

The first 30 minutes of your day/work day/study session should be spent doing work. If you need to check email or your social news sites, do it once you've established a good work flow and you'll find it much easier to shut it off. Or better yet, block distractions out completely until you've finished.

If you find it difficult to jump into those first 30 minutes then tell yourself that you're just going to get 10 minutes of work done, and if it's just too painful you'll give yourself a break. That first 10 minutes is usually all you need to start getting focused.

2) Become more self-aware

Procrastination usually comes in two forms:

1. Difficulty in starting a task
2. Getting distracted while working on a task

You tell yourself, 'I really need to get started on this.'

You feel stressed.

You feel an urge to do something else, so you tell yourself, 'I'll get started soon, but I can afford another five minutes doing this one other thing.'

Giving yourself this little reprieve relieves the stress temporarily and reinforces the neural pathways associated with procrastination, making it just a bit easier to fall prey to procrastination again, five minutes later.

Try this

Next time you find yourself facing this never-ending cycle, next time you're about to start a task and you feel a voice in your head telling you to 'check your email, it might be important!', or 'I wonder if anyone commented on my Facebook status', resist the urge. Tell yourself to wait 15 minutes.

You'll find that the urge does actually pass once you acknowledge it for what it is – a sudden impulse driven by your brain.

Block out distractions

This goes back to willpower and acknowledging that it's a limited resource that can be depleted like any other form of energy. What does this mean for someone trying to get rid of procrastination? It means that just knowing that these social platforms are one click away can make it more likely that you'll get distracted and start procrastinating. While you might be able to resist the temptation during the first half of your work day, as you expend energy focusing you'll become more and more likely to give in to temptation and start procrastinating.

To avoid this, make use of software that can block distracting websites, or block the internet out altogether. Not having to deal with the temptation of constant distractions will not only make it less likely that you'll succumb to momentary temptation, but it will actually give you more energy to focus on your work and avoid procrastinating when you're tired. I recently set an eight-hour block on

Facebook on my work computer so that I cannot check it when I am working – this small step has enabled a much better habit of checking at specific times of day or for whole days not at all!

Another choice I made recently was to take email off my Smartphone completely because I found myself checking it too much over the course of a day. I discovered that I was more productive without it and more balanced too, and still able to keep up with everything.

Take the first step

If you feel stuck and feel you can't get started you need to take action. Can't come up with a perfect first line for your essay or report? Just start writing anything that comes to mind on the topic. Can't think of a topic? Just start writing down anything vaguely related to the subject matter or write a structure instead and start filling in notes on each section or theme. The same can be applied to studying. Is the thought of reading that thick textbook too intimidating? Just start by reading the table of contents, or the first page. Too tired to take notes or really process the concepts? Just skim through what you need to get through and come back tomorrow to re-examine the material when you're refreshed. Getting something done is better than doing nothing, and once you get started you'll often find you have more energy than you thought you did.

Make a date

Human beings can be strange – if we're meeting a friend, we'll set a fixed time to do so, and we show up. Most of us would never make an appointment with a friend and simply avoid showing up for no reason at all. Yet when it comes to important tasks like going to the gym, or getting another section of our dissertation completed, we'll just set vague goals and feel perfectly comfortable pushing back our self-imposed deadlines. Schedule your important tasks and show up every time, no matter what, and you'll see an immediate impact.

So what? How you can use the information in this chapter to boost your skills

This chapter has focused on giving you insights and ideas on how to increase your productivity levels. It is not so much about achieving more in less time but about working smartly to ensure that what you are producing is the very best that you can give. Working smartly will also have an immediate impact on stress levels as well as free up time to create more balance in your life. This balance can mean having time for meeting with friends, leisure activities and even sleep – the very things that perhaps you will tell yourself you do not have time for if you are working to a deadline. It is easy to let these things go, even activities that are essential to our wellbeing like eating nutritional foods that boost our brain. In fact, if anything if we are working very hard we are likely to skip healthy meals, telling ourselves that we do not have time to cook, and we may even justify rewarding ourselves with junk food.

Working smarter is important for your communication skills because you will feel much more equipped to communicate clearly and succinctly. If you are in control over when you send and receive email you are far more likely to write well rather than reactively – we discuss email more in the next chapter. If you are more productive and working efficiently you also feel more in control and this has a direct positive impact on your brain rather than feeling overwhelmed and drowning in to-do lists and information.

Further reading

Baumeister, Roy and Tierney, John. 2012. *Willpower: Why Self-Control is the Secret to Success.* Penguin.

Clipperton, Guy. 2013. *The Smarter Working Manifesto, When, Where and How do you Work Best?* Sunmaker.

Dweck, Carol. 2007. *Mindset: The New Psychology of Success – How We Can Learn to Fulfil Our Potential.* Ballantine.

Kahneman, Daniel. 2011. *Thinking Fast and Slow.* Farrar, Straus and Giroux.

Rubin, Gretchen. 2016. *Better Than Before: What I Learned About Making and Breaking Habits – to Sleep More, Quit Sugar, Procrastinate Less, and Generally Build a Happier Life.* Two Roads.

Steel, Piers. 2011. *The Procrastination Equation: How to Stop Putting Things Off and Start Getting Stuff Done.* Pearson Life.

Effective Email

What's in this chapter:

- Did you know? Facts and statistics about email communication
- Is email communication even necessary?
- Some of the best uses of email
- The irresistible urge to check emails
- The dopamine loop and how to break out of it
- Writing good emails – tips and ideas
- Some email habits to avoid
- Email – what we fail to notice
- So what? How you can use the information in this chapter to produce effective email

Did you know?

Facts and statistics about email communication

- According to an email statistics report conducted by the Radicati Group for 2015–2019, 2.6 billion people used email worldwide as of 2015, each sending and receiving an average of 122 emails a day at work alone. Email is frequently cited as a major drain on productivity. Very few people used email consistently even 20 years ago so email as a form of communication is relatively new.
- Research conducted by The Relevancy Group (Kushlev and Dunn, 2015) reveals that 66% of us check our email account multiple times per day, with 13% of us actually checking email hourly or more frequently.
- According to a report from IDC Research, which examined habits of smartphone users, 79% of adult smartphone users have their phones with them for 22 hours a day and check their mobile devices within 15 minutes of waking up each morning (Lee et al., 2014).

Is email communication even necessary?

Thinking point

There was once a professor in the US whose dean had reprimanded him for trying to teach his students how to write.

The professor, who has been teaching business and law students at some of America's top universities for 50 years, told an MBA class that clear writing would be essential in their careers.

Each week in his class, they would compose a one-page memorandum, which he would read and mark. The memos would answer a simple question from their textbooks. 'I wanted the assignment to be more about conveying their analyses than testing their ability to get the analyses right', he said. Did students appreciate or understand this? 'The students complained so vigorously to the dean that the dean urged me to stop.' The students said that in business today they did not need to know how to write. 'Emails and tweets are the medium of exchange. So, they argued, the constant back-and-forth gives one an opportunity to correct misunderstandings caused by unclear thinking and writing.'

The dean insisted that the professor make the writing exercise voluntary. By the end of the term, only one student, a non-native English speaker, was submitting the assignments.

Source: Skapinker, 2013

What do you think? Some may argue that if a lot of communication is via email it is not necessary to know how to write discourse and convey an argument articulately as the professor was suggesting. Or do you think that with short communications such as email or Twitter that go back and forth you can correct any misunderstandings? Certainly if emails can cause tension, confusion, or other negative consequences then surely good communication is key and as emails are in written format, good writing is surely also important?

Email is used widely as a source of business communication even though how we use email is changing and is likely to shift more to in-company instant messaging platforms for those newly entering the workplace. With the rise of social networks, collaborative tools and mobile devices, email may start to phase out. Whether employees are logging into a community intranet and getting up to speed on the latest conversations, or adding events and meetings to a shared calendar, they are likely to spend more and more time with shared social components outside of their email inboxes.

Until relatively recently, email was indeed used for everything from sending documents to communicating across time zones. It is still used a great deal in the workplace and is the main form of communication for most tasks.

How email impacts organisational culture

Imagine a typical day at work starting in the morning with a cup of coffee, greeting your colleagues and then the inevitable happens, you log in on your computer. For many organisations, not realising that it is dominating the rest of the office day, this simple action has become automatic behaviour. Emails constantly ask for attention and intrude into our working schedule. The LinkedIn profile needs an update, one has to respond to messages on the discussion board, scan the company network for news messages, etc. Only a few have the discipline to structure the day in such a way that they plan fixed times to deal with email. Remarkably, the answering of email is rarely part of any job description, but more an underlying assumption of the functioning in organisational life nowadays.

The original idea of email, though, was to make organisational life easier and to facilitate more effective communication. The impact of email on a typical workday, though, is inherent in differences between email and face-to-face communication. McKenna and Bargh (2000) listed these differences in four categories:

1) Physical distance is no issue on the internet; in a fraction of a second one can interact with someone at the other end of the world.
2) This can be an influential cue in interpreting a message. When a colleague sends you an email at 2am you put it in another perspective than when you receive the same message at 10am. The internet is a speedy medium that allows us to reach a large group of people in one delivery.
3) Physical appearance and visual cues are absent in email.
4) It is easier to be anonymous while communicating on the internet. It is common to use nicknames in chat devices and pseudonyms are used in the construction of email accounts.

In the workplace there is an implicit expectation to respond to emails and rapidly. There isn't necessarily any reward or bonus for doing so and most of the time email takes away from the actual work set out in a job description.

Some organisations recognise that overuse of email and constantly checking email impacts job performance and some companies have email 'policies'. These policies may include when to use email (with some companies adopting a strict 'no evening and weekend emails' rule), appropriate content, guidance on how to write email, use of password-protected accounts, use of company email signatures, email etiquette and managing information overload. However, there is no standard for such policies and so practices will differ from workplace to workplace with many companies still adopting an 'always on' culture.

Here are some of the best uses of email

- Email works well when you want to ask a question or deliver a message quickly and it is not necessarily important how fast you get your answer – or even if you will get a reply. Email is a wonderful way to send a quick message, but it is not necessarily the best route to a quick reply so it's important to think about when a meeting or phone call may be more effective.
- If you want to communicate directly with a particular person in an organisation rather than fight your way past a gatekeeper, email can be effective. As long as you have the correct email address, chances are your message will be read by your intended recipient. However, it may not work well if this is an unsolicited

request or the recipient does not know you as the company email system may well have strong spam filters in place, which may mean your email will not get seen.

- Email can work well when you need to communicate with someone in a different time zone or country. You can still send and receive email within working hours. However, there can still be an expectation to be sending and receiving emails outside working hours as time zones become blurred.
- Because email is electronic, you can easily deliver the same message to multiple readers. Whether it's a memo for the five other members of your team or an electronic newsletter with 10,000 subscribers, email makes it easy to deliver news quickly, easily, and at no cost. However, more recently data protection laws have come into play which means that recipients will need to be able to subscribe to your newsletter or opt out. Add to this the fact that your newsletter may be competing with many other similar types of email. For sending information out to a team it may well be more effective to use collaboration software.
- Email is valuable if you need to maintain a written record of your electronic conversation. Of course, this can also work the other way which is why it is important to write email well. Every email you send is potentially visible to a wide number of people if forwarded on as well as serving as a written record.
- When it's urgent. If something is due at 8am, you can work late at night and still deliver it on time using email. While it's possible that there will be technical problems in the transmission, most emails are delivered without a hitch.
- Email is good for providing factual information that does not necessarily require an answer. For example, a price quote or to tell someone what time an event starts.
- Email can be good for sending requested documents or as follow-up to a meeting or call. While it is not polite to send large unrequested attachments, email is easy for quickly delivering requested items.

Email can certainly be very efficient but because there are no clear rules for email etiquette, messages can be composed and written in a variety of ways and can range from short, abrupt communications to very long missives. There are also no standard rules about how to start or sign off an email and so many emails can come across as too informal.

The irresistible urge to check emails

Let's not forget that most of us will feel compelled to check our emails several times a day and first thing in the morning. If we know that there are email messages piling up in our inbox we will have an urge to check them and the more often we check them the stronger the urge becomes. Why is this? Remember our friend dopamine? Dopamine is created in various parts of the brain and is critical in all sorts of brain functions, including thinking, moving, sleeping, mood, attention, motivation, seeking and reward. So dopamine controls the pleasure systems of the brain. It used to be thought that dopamine was causing us to experience pleasure but actually what dopamine does is *cause* pleasure-seeking behaviour. Dopamine causes you to want, desire, seek out, and search. It increases your general level of arousal and your goal-directed behaviour.

The dopamine loop

With the internet, Twitter, instant messaging and texting you now have almost instant gratification of your desire to seek. Want to talk to someone right away? Send a text and generally they respond in a few seconds. Want to look up some information or check a random question that just popped into your head? Just type your request into Google. Want to see what your colleagues are up to? Go to LinkedIn. It is so easy to get into what is known as a dopamine-induced loop, which often happens in the workplace too. Dopamine starts you seeking and then you get rewarded for the seeking which in turn makes you seek more. It becomes harder and harder to stop looking at email, stop texting, or stop checking your phone to see if you have a message or a new text. Dopamine is also stimulated by unpredictability. When something happens that is not exactly predictable, that stimulates the dopamine system. Our emails and tweets and texts show up, but we don't know exactly when they will, or who will have sent them. It's unpredictable and this is exactly what stimulates our dopamine system.

Here are some ideas for how to get out of the loop:

Turn off the cues

This is one of the most important things you can do to prevent or stop a dopamine loop and to be more productive: turn off the cues. Adjust the settings on your mobile device and on your laptop, desktop or tablet so that you don't receive the automatic notifications. Those automatic notifications are actually causing you to be like a rat in a cage. If you want to get work done you need to turn off as many auditory and visual cues as possible. It's the best way to prevent and break the dopamine loops. One of the most effective things I have ever done (and I only did it recently and in the course of writing this book) is to switch off email on my phone. It has been a big breakthrough for me and has stopped me from checking email so often. It has made no difference at all to my ability to respond to or write email when I need to but it has made a huge difference to stopping the dopamine loop that I had started to be part of. It also means that
I use commuter time or travel time to work rather than respond to or write email.

If we can learn to switch off our smartphones and check email only at designated points in the day this will have an immediate impact on the brain and also make us more effective. Doing this also impacts how we communicate via email too. The problem with responding to emails as soon as they arrive is that we take less time to reflect and think about how we are responding. Because there is also a perceived expectation that emails 'must be' (why?) responded to immediately we may fire off a response that might be inappropriate, badly thought out or not even needed. Even worse, our brain isn't able to distinguish between the relative importance of our emails so that they all become important. Mix that with social media and you have a lethal cocktail of the brain constantly reacting and communicating less effectively. Both Chapters 2 and 3, about overcoming distractions and working smarter, touch on the subject of controlling our environment and our technology. Doing this also makes a powerful difference to *how* we communicate using this medium as we become far less reactive and more reflective in our approaches and responses.

So the first step to communicating effectively by email is to control our environment so that we are more effective *when* we write. Rather than focusing on email techniques and email etiquette (though also important), controlling your environment is probably the most important thing you can do to help you write email really well!

Self-check

For one day, monitor how often you check your mobile device and your email.

There are useful apps that can help you measure how often you do. Why not download one of these to track your usage? You may be surprised by the results.

You may not receive a lot of email so for you right now it may not be so important to use filters for incoming mail, but why not get familiar with these settings on the email system you use? Having different folders for different types of messages and separating personal from study or work-related messages will also have an immediate impact on your ability to control incoming mails. That way you can batch your email and decide exactly when you want to respond to personal emails and when to respond to work-related ones. Don't be fooled by the notion that if it's work-related your response needs to be immediate! Checking once or twice a day will be sufficient, I promise! It's not easy to do this for all the reasons already mentioned and not least because you will likely be surrounded by people who are doing the exact opposite and expect you to do the same. When I first started to check email less I used to get messages saying, 'Did you receive my email?' and so I had to explain that I check email at certain points of the day only. As long as there is a response within a reasonable time period, your email recipients will soon adapt.

Experiment with scheduling when you check email and turn off your notification settings. This may feel quite odd at first but it's important for you to become much more acutely aware of how you are using technology in order to be able to control it. Otherwise you really are very much like a rat in a cage and you are, like it or not, being controlled by your environment rather than the other way around. Remember that technology is an excellent servant but a very poor master.

Writing effective emails

For those who do it well, email is a near-instant deliverer of information and is an effective communication tool for sending documents and summarising information, setting up meetings and introductions and for generally getting things done. If you consider how you write and send it you can do a lot to lessen the burden of email. That means making your initial message effective and clear, employing short graphs, bulleted points and subheadings. Did you know that a typical conversation on email can include up to seven notes? Making that initial message effective means fewer follow-ups, which will help unclog your inbox as well as your time. However, if something is potentially controversial or complicated, it's not for email.

Because email is so quick and easy it has almost become too popular and some people take the informality of email to extremes with many misspellings and missed out words, which reflect badly on the writer. Because email does not allow you to show tone of voice it is far easier for misunderstandings to arise so some emails can come across as blunt and aggressive, often unintentionally. Even though email is a form of written communication it encourages people to behave impulsively and thoughtlessly because of the dopamine triggers outlined above so first things first: although seemingly instant do not treat email like other forms of instant messaging.

Some email habits to avoid

1) Overuse of the cc button
Be very cautious about who you decide to copy into any email. Think carefully about the recipients before you press send and really think about who needs to get this email and who needs to read it. Copying lots of people into an email, i.e. the entire team just to cover your bases, is not a good idea. Copying in people to update them on information almost always leads to confusion and more emails to clear the confusion. The person who is copied in wonders if they need to take action. Should they respond? Should they forward your email? A 'cc'd' email usually contains information that most people won't be able to process anyway.

Another habit to avoid, when you receive an email with multiple people copied in, is not to automatically send your own answer to everyone! All this does is clog up everyone's inbox. It is far more effective to answer only the person concerned. The email trail does not necessarily need to become a group discussion, however compelling it may feel to 'cover your bases' (and it will be!).

2) Always replying
Not necessary! If communication is complete and everything is clear there is no need to send one final confirmation or final message. Remember you want to reduce the number of possible follow-ups and long email trails where important information can get lost.

3) Badly written subject lines
The subject line should be selected thoughtfully. Try to give as many details as you can in the shortest format possible. For example: 'Meeting 02/15 Documents'. When receiving the email, your correspondent needs to understand what your email is about just by reading its subject line. Do not make them guess what's inside; be explicit and concise. This also avoids people responding to your email with a completely different subject simply because an email from you has popped up and something has occurred to them that they

need to let you know about. And beware of doing the same thing yourself. This happens so often and can become really confusing.

4) **Using capital letters**

Using CAPITAL letters will not make your email more urgent than others. In an email, capitalised letters are generally interpreted as aggressive and intrusive and they do little to build a constructive conversation. If you do want to flag your email as urgent think carefully about when you do this and why, and only use the red 'high importance' flag if it really is of high importance.

5) **Not prioritising your answers**

Not every email needs to be answered right away. So it is a good idea to classify and prioritise them accordingly. The problem is, your inbox is the worst tool to use. An external application will be more effective for using those mailbox filters I mentioned earlier. The perfect email is an email that can be deleted; it is not supposed to hold information or store it for you. You need to prioritise your answers in a to-do list and transfer the information that an email contains to another place.

6) **Using unnecessary words**

Just like your email subject line, your email body should be very explicit and concise. Go straight to the point and avoid as much unnecessary or additional information as possible as this will only lead to the need for more follow-up and clarification. Most people don't read everything in their emails, so if you facilitate the job by giving short useful information, by bulleting your content and by saying which actions should be taken, you are saving everyone a lot of time.

7) **Using email for everything**

Whether you need to say something to someone, to send information and documents, to share an idea and gather feedback, to plan an event or to synchronise your team, try not to automatically resort to email every time. Think about the message you want to deliver, and use the right tool for each specific message. Emails are not always the right medium to communicate what you need. You may want to use a social media platform or a project management app instead.

8) **Managing a team project by email**

Managing a team project with email can often lead to frustration, misunderstanding, confusion and in the end, a bad outcome. When you're organising a team project, you need to delegate tasks, share information and follow up on everyone's work. But emails are just a way to communicate, not to plan. Change your habits and find a better way to manage your teamwork without email! There are plenty of good project management tools out there that will be far more effective than email.

Try this

Take a look at the following communication needs and decide which ones are suitable for email and which ones might be better suited to another medium and if so, which one:

Communication need	Medium to use
Sending out some key information as a follow-up to a meeting	
An initial response to an employment opportunity	
Giving some bad news to a friend	
Getting input from your team about an upcoming project	
Letting your colleagues know about a work social get-together	
Sending a presentation in advance of an upcoming conference event	
Sending a personal message	
Sending a thank you message	

There are no right or wrong answers to these and your answers should probably reflect a mix of email, telephone, team software, messaging and maybe even a handwritten letter for the thank you note! The important thing here is to be aware of when to use email. Too often it is easy to hide behind email or fire off messages thinking they will be read or interpreted the way that we want them to be.

Email – what we fail to notice

Unlike face-to-face communication we have no way of reading any environmental cues when it comes to email. We have no way of knowing how our message will be received and it can be difficult to practise or make use of empathy. When speaking face-to-face, it's the verbal and nonverbal social cues that allow us to gauge the best way to arrange our wording in order to get our point across clearly. In email, we don't get such real-time feedback. Once our message is in the hand of the recipient, we've lost all control. This is why it is so important to think carefully about how your email is composed and whether or not it is even the right medium to be using in the first place.

What can happen with email is that all too often we become fixated on the knowledge we wish to impart, and we shift our attention off the reader and what he or she really wants to know.

There is now software that can analyse your language patterns and social interaction in order to improve your email communication in real time. This is in response to the increase of email misuse and misinterpretation of emails. But equally, paying more attention to the way you send (encode) your email messages and also to how you read (decode) your messages will go a long way towards better email communication. It requires a little slowing down and a little more reflection but it can definitely be done!

What is 'empathy'?

Not to be confused with sympathy, empathy is the conscious action of being aware of, and sensitive to, someone else's feelings, thoughts and experiences; and not judging them through your own lens. Empathy is demonstrated through active listening and being fully present when someone is communicating with you rather than jumping in with your own thoughts, assumptions, impressions or perceptions.

Although harder to do in an email, it can be done. Taking some time to really think about how a message might be received may help you to revise some of the language you use – it's easy to tap out a quick response that can come across as terse or abrupt, even angry in an email without you intending it to. If you know the person you are emailing, think about how they might wish to receive messages; be polite, be clear and be kind!

Basic principles for effective emails

Don't over-communicate by email

One of the biggest sources of stress at work is the sheer volume of emails that people receive. So, before you begin writing an email, ask yourself: 'Is this really necessary? Might a phone call or meeting face-to-face be more effective?' Remember too that a poorly written email can result in those seven extra emails to seek clarification. You may want to use the phone or instant messaging to deal with any questions that are likely to need some back-and-forth discussion. It is also important to be aware that email is not as secure as you might want it to be, particularly as people may forward emails without thinking to delete the conversation history. Always avoid sharing sensitive or personal information in an email, and avoid writing about anything that you, or the subject of your email, would not like to see made public by your office or your network of contacts.

If the content of your email is potentially negative, or could be perceived that way, think instead about how you might resolve this matter by speaking in person. This will help you to communicate with empathy, compassion and understanding; these can be lost behind email.

How to write a good subject line

A newspaper headline has two functions: it grabs your attention, and it summarises the article so that you can decide whether to read it or not. The subject line of your email message should do the same thing. A blank subject line is more likely to be overlooked or rejected as 'spam', so always use a few well-chosen words to tell the recipient what the email is about.

You may want to include the date in the subject line if your message is one of a regular series of emails, such as a weekly project report. For a message that needs a response, you might also want to include a call to action, such as 'Please reply by 7 November'.

A well-written subject line delivers the most important information, without the recipient even having to open the email. This serves as a prompt that reminds recipients about your meeting every time they glance at their inbox. For more, see the table and the questions that follow.

Subject line 1	Subject line 2
Subject: Meeting	**Subject:** PASS Process Meeting – 10am, 14 March, 20--.

Try this ✎

Take a look at the two subject lines above. Which is the clearer message?

Subject line 2 gives the recipient clear and concise information about the meeting right in the subject line whereas Subject line 1 is really too vague and runs the risk of not even being opened!

> **TIP**
> If you have a very short message to convey, and you can fit the whole thing into the subject line, use 'EOM' (End of Message) to let recipients know that they don't need to open the email to get all the information that they need. For example:
>
> **Subject:** Could you please send the February sales report? Thanks! EOM
>
> Of course, this is only useful if recipients know what 'EOM' means and some companies will have internal policies and acronyms about this so do check this first!

Keep messages clear and brief

Emails, like traditional business letters, need to be clear and concise so keep your sentences short and to the point. The body of the email should be direct and informative, and it should contain all pertinent information.

Unlike traditional letters, however, it costs no more to send several emails than it does to send just one. So, if you need to communicate with someone about a number of different topics, consider writing a separate email for each one. This makes your message clearer, and it allows your correspondent to reply to one topic at a time.

Quick check: study this example below:

> **Subject: Revisions for Sales Report**
>
> Hi Jackie,
>
> Thanks for sending that report last week. I read it yesterday, and I feel that Section 2 needs more specific information about our sales figures. I also felt that the tone could be more formal.
>
> Also, I wanted to let you know that I've scheduled a meeting with the PR department for this Friday regarding the new ad campaign. It's at 11.00am and will be in the small conference room. Please let me know if you can make that time.
>
> Thanks!
> Monica

There are too many topics within the same email which means that the receiver is getting mixed messages and will find it difficult to respond. This happens a lot more than you may think, simply because the writer is thinking of several things, that are relevant for the recipient and decides to put them all into one message while they are in his/her mind. However, doing this will only result in a trail of emails back and forth.

Contrast the example above with the following reworked email:

Subject: Revisions for Sales Report

Hi Jackie,

Thanks for sending that report last week. I read it yesterday, and I feel that Section 2 needs more specific information about our sales figures.

I also felt that the tone could be more formal. Please could you amend it with these comments in mind?

Thanks for your hard work on this!

Monica

(Monica then follows this up with a separate email about the PR department meeting.)

It is important to find balance here. You don't want to bombard someone with emails, and it can make sense to combine several, related, points into one email. When this happens, keep things simple with numbered paragraphs or bullet points, and consider 'chunking' information into small, well-organised units to make it easier to digest.

Notice, too, that in the good example above, Monica specified what she wanted Jackie to do (in this case, amend the report). If you make it easy for people to see what you want, there's a better chance that they will give you what you want and it is good to end an email with a clear action point if one is needed.

Be polite

People often think that emails are less formal than traditional letters. But the messages you send are still a reflection of your own professionalism, values and attention to detail, so a certain level of formality is needed in the workplace. Unfortunately, email can also be used to hide behind if the content or topic is potentially negative so again, always consider whether a phone call or meeting may be more effective.

Unless you're on good terms with someone, avoid informal language, slang, jargon and inappropriate abbreviations. Emoticons can be useful for clarifying your intent, but it really is best to use them only with people you know well.

Close your message with 'Regards', 'Yours sincerely', 'Best wishes' or 'All the best', depending on the situation. Again, there is no standardised ending to an email so you will need to select one that fits the context and the nature of the relationship.

Check the tone

When we meet people face-to-face, we use the other person's body language, vocal tone, and facial expressions to assess how they feel. Email takes this information and important environmental cues away, and means that we can't really tell when people may have misunderstood or misinterpreted our messages.

Your choice of words, sentence length, punctuation and capitalisation can easily be misinterpreted without visual and auditory cues. In the first example below, Emma might think that Harry is frustrated or angry, but, in reality, he feels fine.

Emma,

I need your report by 5pm today or I'll miss my deadline.

Harry

If Emma does interpret this message to mean that Harry is angry this may have repercussions when they subsequently see each other offline. Again, this can happen more than you may think so we need to take more care over email to minimise the chance for misinterpretation. Equally when we are on the receiving end of emails we need to check in with ourselves before jumping to unnecessary conclusions about what the email means.

Contrast Harry's first message with the following one and there is much less room for misinterpretation:

Hi Emma,

Thanks for all your hard work on that report. Could you please get your version over to me by 5pm, so I don't miss my deadline?

Thanks so much!

Harry

Think about how your email 'feels' emotionally. If your intentions or emotions could be misunderstood, find a less ambiguous way to phrase your words.

Always proofread

Finally, before you hit 'send', take a moment to review your email for spelling, grammar and punctuation mistakes. Your email messages are as much a part of your professional image as the clothes you wear, so it looks bad to send out a message that contains typos.

As you proofread, pay careful attention to the length of your email. People are more likely to read short, concise emails than long, rambling ones, so make sure that your emails are as short as possible, without excluding necessary information.

Key points

Most of us are likely to spend a significant portion of our workday reading and composing emails. But the messages we send can be confusing to others.

To write effective emails, first ask yourself if you should be using email at all. Sometimes, it might be better to pick up the phone.

Make your emails concise and to the point. Only send them to the people who really need to see them, and be clear about what you would like the recipient to do next.

Remember that your emails are a reflection of your professionalism, values and attention to detail. Try to imagine how others might interpret the tone of your message. Be polite, and always proofread what you have written before you click 'send'.

Putting it into practice

To practise writing good clear subject headers try looking at a relevant article from a newspaper or magazine. Summarise it in six (or three, or one) bullet point(s). Look at the headline in the article. Turn it into a subject header of not more than four words. Get into the habit of summarising information succinctly.

Try 'format-hopping', using different media for different purposes. For example, invite friends to a social event by email, phone, text message and instant messaging. Compare the responses you get in each format!

Get into the habit of writing email if you don't normally use this medium. Use your knowledge of the communication process to compose your email thinking about tone, the recipient, clarity of message and polite sign-off.

If you receive emails from others, look at the way they are written too. Yes, you will get emails that are poorly written, too informal or direct and open to misinterpretation. Always respond politely and clearly. Do not fall into the common trap of firing emails back and forth, especially if the message is prone to be negative: resist any urge to fire off a quick response and press 'send'.

Finally, it's worth noting that many companies are slowly beginning to move away from email towards using instant messaging for the following reasons:

- Instant messaging allows teams to communicate more easily. Email, simply, is not very efficient for long discussions or large groups. Instant messaging easily facilitates a far shorter discussion with quicker back-and-forth replies. People also tend to be more spontaneous when they don't have time to overly think through their words and this is believed to allow for more original thought and honest viewpoints. Chat rooms and instant messaging platforms also allow everyone to add their input. Because of this, their ideas and viewpoints are not lost in a reply chain.

- Instant messaging (IM) is conversational. This kind of communication has an immediate back-and-forth exchange that lets you collaborate in real time. The value of this in brainstorming and planning sessions is immeasurable. As noted above, IM exchanges tend to be shorter and less self-censored. This lets teams bring together multiple ideas and viewpoints on everything from projects to planning sessions for new ideas.

- Email can feel largely impersonal, and particularly because of the disconnect of an instantaneous response. You, as the new generation of employees, are likely to want to be part of a team and to know that your ideas are heard, acknowledged and respected. Through the use of instant messaging, employees are able to more effectively communicate and thus form the types of bonds and camaraderie upon which all good teams are built.

So what? How you can use the information in this chapter to produce effective email

This chapter has focused on one aspect of business communication – writing effective email. Email may or may not be something you are currently using a great deal and it is partly because of this that it is so important for you to have a good understanding of how email is used, as well as how badly it is used, so as to develop great email habits. Writing email should be efficient and something that boosts your productivity, rather than being a drain on it (which it so often is). It can also be a great way to communicate provided it is used appropriately. It can clinch the decision to give you a job, in that a well-written email will determine if the receiver wants to open the attachment that is your CV or disregard your message because of its tone or spelling errors. Email can often be the very first impression that someone has of you so it needs to be as good as possible. Most of all, don't hide behind email. If you feel something is probably better said face-to-face, then it probably is.

Further reading

Fisher, Janis. 2015. *E-mail: A Write It Well Guide: How to Write and Manage E-mail in the Workplace.* Advanced Communications Design Inc.

Rubin, Danny. 2015. *Wait, How Do I Write This Email: Game-Changing Templates for Networking and the Job Search.* News to Live By.

Wright, Heather. 2015. *A Quick Guide to Writing Better Emails (Better Business Communication).* CreateSpace Independent Publishing Platform.

Face-to-Face Communication

What's in this chapter:

- Did you know? Facts and statistics about face-to-face communication
- The power of face-to-face
- The role of emotional cues in face-to-face communication
- Embracing empathy
- Reading faces and active listening
- What you don't say
- So what? How you can use the information in this chapter to improve your face-to-face communication

---

Did you know?

Facts and statistics about face-to-face communication

- Research from MIT's Human Dynamics Laboratory (Pentland, 2012) shows that face-to-face meetings allow members to come up with more ideas and become more capable as a group compared to virtual meetings.
- You might argue that you can still 'read' a person's facial expressions over video chat, but some things can still get lost in translation. Of brainstorming sessions done face-to-face, over the phone or via video chat, the face-to-face sessions tend to produce significantly more creative ideas.
- Most of face-to-face communication has subtle emotional cues that can be challenging to pick up, but when we do make us far more effective communicators.
- We register basic emotions of disgust, anger, fear, joy and anxiety within milliseconds, before we even open our mouths.

The power of face-to-face

You are unique – there is only one of you and when it comes to face-to-face communication you are your own best asset. It makes sense to focus on how we communicate in person because it is probably going to be one of the best methods we have in an over-communicated and over-stimulated world. Your offline persona needs to be fully aligned with your online one, though! In today's world it is possible to go through an entire day without dealing with anyone in person, such is our reliance on online communication, but face-to-face communication and in-person meetings can actually boost efficiency much more than we think and have considerable benefits in terms of enhancing relationships and even saving time.

Instead of spending an entire day emailing or messaging back and forth, you can clarify the details of something or work out how to best tackle a project more efficiently in person – it may feel easier to use messaging or email but rarely is communication as effective. Face-to-face meetings also boost creativity as overall energy tends to be higher which means you are more likely to brainstorm and solve a multitude of problems at a time. Communication becomes much richer and fuller as a result and relationships are improved. We often underestimate the power of human interaction because we are so focused on the speed of communication. And as much as the power of technology allows us to video conference, produce a CV on YouTube along with a presentation or interact virtually in real time, nothing is of higher value than face-to-face communication.

Probably one of the biggest advantages to face-to-face communication is our ability to accurately read and respond to nonverbal cues which is impossible online. You can gauge how interested someone is in what you are talking about by reading their body language. If you are in a meeting and your fellow team members are fiddling with their pens, or checking their watches, you know that you have to either adjust the tone of your voice or use more exciting language to capture their attention. Likewise, if they are actively nodding their heads and smiling, it is clear that they are engaged with you and your message. It is the same with presentations and other interactions. When you interact online, however, you have no way of reading these cues nor of knowing how attentive your audience is and messages have more propensity to be misinterpreted. Addressing these misunderstandings can take longer than taking the time to meet face-to-face.

The research picture

Researchers from Beijing Normal University (Jiang et al., 2012) point out that face-to-face communication differs from other forms of communication in two key ways:

1) Face-to-face communication involves the integration of 'multimodal sensory information', such as nonverbal cues (facial expressions and physical gestures).
2) Face-to-face communication involves more continuous turn-taking behaviours between partners and this has been shown to play a pivotal role in social interactions and reflects the level of involvement of a person in the communication.

These factors are critical to effective communication and may even play a role in helping to synchronise your brain with others during a conversation. In fact, there is a significant increase in the neural synchronisation between the brains of two people during face-to-face, but not during other types of, conversation.

Researchers studying human conversation have discovered the brains of listeners and speakers become synchronised, and this 'neural coupling' makes for effective communication. In essence, the participants' brains connect in a kind of 'mind meld'.

According to the study (Jiang et al., 2012), which was published in *The Journal of Neuroscience*:

> These results suggest that face-to-face communication, particularly dialogue, has special neural features that other types of communication do not have and that the neural synchronisation between partners may underlie successful face-to-face communication.

The **quality** of the communication was found to be a more important contributor to neural synchronisation than the **quantity** of communication. This suggests that perhaps even infrequent in-person meetings may have more of an impact than frequent digital meetings.

Psychologist Uri Hasson wanted to find out which areas of the brain were active during speaking and listening in a conversation to test a hypothesis that there is more overlap between these brain areas than is generally assumed (Princeton University Institute, 2014). It has been noted, for example, that people taking part in conversations will often subconsciously imitate each other's grammar, rates of speaking and even gestures and posture.

Brain-to-Brain coupling: A mechanism for creating and sharing a social world (Uri Hasson, Asif A. Ghazanfar, Bruno Galantucci, Simon Garrod, Christian Keysers Trends Cogn Sci. 2012 Feb;16(2):114–21)

"In the first part of the experiment, a graduate student placed her head in a functional magnetic resonance imaging (fMRI) machine for 15 minutes, while she recounted an unrehearsed story from her school years. The research team recorded the story using a microphone capable of filtering out the noise of the fMRI machine, and then in the second part of the experiment a number of volunteers had their heads scanned by the fMRI machine while listening to the recording.

The team found a great deal of synchronisation between the activity in the student's brain and in those of the 11 volunteers, with the same regions of the brains lighting up at or near the same points in the story. This finding was surprising, given the long-held belief that speaking and listening use separate areas of the brain. The areas of the brain affected were linked to language, but their exact functions are as yet unknown.

In most areas of the brain the activation pattern appeared one to three seconds after it had appeared in the student's brain, but in a few other areas, including an area in the frontal lobe, the activation pattern appeared in the listeners' brains before it appeared in the student's, which the researchers thought could represent the listeners anticipating what was coming next in the story.

The researchers then asked the subjects to re-tell the story they had heard, and found there was a positive correlation between the strength of the neural coupling and the volunteer's ability to recall the story details. Hasson concluded that the 'more similar our brain patterns during a conversation, the better we understand each other'." The results are published in the *Proceedings of the National Academy of Sciences* journal and the paper is available online.

The role of emotional cues in face-to-face communication

The point here is that in face-to-face communication it isn't just your words that count but also what you don't say. Whether that is communicated via body language or facial expressions, verbal plus nonverbal give us a much more complete picture of a message. Even if we are not making any conscious effort we are constantly receiving messages from the world around us and in the same way we are always communicating something to other people, whether we mean to or not. Everything we do is a form of communication even when we are not saying a word. How we feel about other people and ourselves will also influence consciously, or unconsciously, how we communicate. In fact, the famous ratio of nonverbal communication to verbal by Albert Mehrabian and Morton Wiener is often misquoted, as what they were actually referring to was emotion.

The research picture

According to Mehrabian and Wiener, interpersonal communication regarding the communication model consists of three elements:

- words spoken – that which is literally being said
- intonation – how something is said (use of voice)
- body language – which posture, facial expressions and gestures someone uses.

This persistent myth comes from a common misrepresentation of research conducted by Mehrabian and Wiener in the 1960s about how much the communication of feelings and attitudes – likes and dislikes – depends on the words, tone of voice and facial expressions or body language. The experiments themselves were conducted on a very small and uniform sample of volunteers and tested just single words with only the face visible, so it is difficult to extract any meaningful figure from the research. But one thing is clear: this is not about communicating information, it is about communicating feelings.

So how you *feel* about someone or a situation is just as important as what you say and how you say it and each of these will have a bearing on your message. It's important to understand this as otherwise it will be tempting to project your feelings and emotions about a situation or person onto your communications, something we can do all too easily.

Meeting face-to-face builds trust

Meeting in person allows for increased eye contact, which builds increased trust and encourages group members to confide in and co-create with their group. Research published in the *International Journal of Organisational Design and Engineering* (Gloor et al., 2012) found:

[T]he more team members directly interact with each other face-to-face, and the more they trust other team members, the more creative and of higher quality the result of their teamwork is. (*Int. J. Organisational Design and Engineering*, Vol. 2, No. 4, 2012)

The power of face-to-face meetings has not been lost on some of the most successful corporations in the world. The late Steve Jobs, founder of Apple, is said to have designed workspaces in order to force people to have more in-person interactions.

Google also serves its employees free food in cafeterias, in part to encourage them to stay on campus and mingle with their co-workers over lunch. Yahoo even made headlines in 2013 for, controversially, banning telecommuting for its employees (Tkaczyk, 2013). At the time, Yahoo CEO Marissa Mayer stated:

Some of the best decisions and insights come from hallway and cafeteria discussions, meeting new people, and impromptu team meetings. Speed and quality are often sacrificed when we work from home. We need to be one Yahoo!, and that starts with physically being together. (In Swisher, 2013)

In a way this is nothing new. It makes sense that higher-value interaction, including more ideas and better decisions, come from face-to-face conversations rather than from behind a screen.

Embracing empathy

Daniel Pink argues in his book *A Whole New Mind* (2011) that empathy is one of six areas vital to success today. Empathy is a right-brain (interpersonal) quality necessary for communicating well in person. Without empathy we will lack strong listening skills or the ability to truly respect others and value their opinions. Empathy is also referred to as 'social intelligence'. Socially intelligent people are able to assess more quickly the emotions of those around them and adapt their words, responses, tones and gestures accordingly. This is important more than ever before as we are called upon to collaborate with larger groups of people in different settings, both virtual and non-virtual. In a truly globally connected world, your skill set could see you working in any number of locations or having work colleagues from very different backgrounds. You will need to be able to operate in whatever environment or cultural context you find yourself. This demands specific abilities, such as language skills, but also an ability to adapt to, sense and respond to changing circumstances and new contexts.

We naturally find empathy difficult because we tend to look at everything from our own perspective. If you are discussing a friend's personal situation you are very likely also to be looking at it from your own perspective and how you would feel and what you would do if you lost your job or relationship or didn't get the interview you wanted.

Try this

> Next time a friend is telling you about a personal situation try out some active listening skills. These can be as simple as asking more questions (to understand more fully), being focused and present rather than thinking about what you will say next, and maintaining eye contact and engaged body language.

Active listening is a key facet of empathy and these listening skills can be strengthened and developed.

We need to get better at reading people's faces and body language and that means simply paying far more attention to people we are interacting with than we would normally do. Facial expressions actually reveal the real feelings underneath which are perhaps not being voiced. They are visible for only a few seconds but long enough for you to recognise quite easily as long as you pay attention and are not distracted by your own thoughts.

Active listening will have a dramatic impact on your conversations and interactions. Although this skill is hard work and requires effort it can be put into practice in virtually any situation with immediate effect!

There are four kinds of listening; you will easily recognise these because either you will have been on the receiving end or you will do at least one of them yourself:

1. **Pretending to listen** – 'yeah, uh huh, right'
2. **Selective** – tuning in and out
3. **Attentive** – paying attention to the words being said so that you can repeat them, but not necessarily understanding the message
4. **Empathic** – listening with the intent to understand – and that is active listening

Because we tend to listen with ourselves in mind most of the time, we are likely to respond in one of four typical ways when others tell us something:

1. We **evaluate** – we decide if we agree or disagree

2. We **probe** – asking questions to clarify

3. We **advise** – giving counsel based on our personal experience: 'Give it some time, it'll be OK'

4. We **interpret** – we try to explain others' behaviours and motives: 'You're just angry now, it'll be fine later on'

Self-check

Think about the last conversation you had – it may have been this morning or quite recently. Can you identify which kind of listening you did and how you responded? Remember that the more you can raise your awareness of how you listen the more quickly you can tap into actively listening.

Here are two ways you can practise active listening – try them the very next time you have a conversation and see what happens:

Being interested in what the other person is saying, with a readiness and ability to listen. Now, you may not actually *be* interested initially, but, curiously, by acting interested we start to become interested. How do you show interest? By using positive body language (eye contact, open stance, mirroring their body language) and reflecting back to the other person what is being said, and also by asking lots of questions.

Being present. Most of the time, when others are speaking, we are focused on what we are going to say next or on our own thoughts and we are less likely to be anchored in the present moment. You may have to force yourself to be present but when you are it pays huge dividends.

Try this

The very next time you communicate with someone, set aside your own need (and be prepared for that need to be quite strong!) to say the next thing, and genuinely seek to understand first. Don't push, be patient, be respectful, understand their emotions, clarify their statements and be discerning, sensitive and aware.

Just try it the next time you are talking to a friend or family member. You will see an immediate change, either in the direction your conversation takes or the outcome as a result of that conversation.

Total immersion

Another way to develop empathy is to try and totally and completely immerse ourselves in what it might feel like to walk in another person's shoes. This is hard to do and takes effort because it means consciously directing our awareness to something our mind does not naturally gravitate towards. That's because our sense of individuality and ego is so very strong and ingrained. But it *is* possible! It's possible through very consciously focusing on another person and stepping outside of ourselves; through really listening and making sure we understand.

Try this

Try practising this kind of focus in an everyday situation and notice the effect it has. If you want to raise your awareness even more, keep a mini-journal of your experience over a few days. Here's an example: you go into your local bank to pay in some money or to ask a question. There's a long queue and you are in a hurry. Finally, you get to the window. Instead of conducting the transaction in a hurry and barely looking at the person behind the counter, perhaps inwardly blaming the bank and by default the person serving you, you smile and ask how he/she is and maybe even acknowledge the wait. The effect can be transformational and you will certainly feel a lot happier and less stressed as a result. You can transfer this kind of scenario to any situation where there is propensity for stress or for responding in auto-pilot.

Most of the time we focus our attention only on ourselves. Every single experience you have, from standing in line at the bank to attending a project meeting or study group, is undertaken through our own personal lens and it will be the same in the workplace too. Try doing this a different way. It will feel like work and might even feel exhausting but it does have an immediate impact.

Just why is empathy so powerful?

Psychologically, empathy is crucial as it meets the critical human need of personal affirmation. After physical survival our greatest human need is psychological survival – that is to be understood, to be validated and appreciated. So when you listen empathetically you are actually giving that person psychological affirmation of their value as a person. That's why it works every time.

Building empathy can happen simply by paying more attention, asking questions, building trust and really listening. A key to this is being fully present in that moment with that other person. Practising mindfulness can also help with cultivating empathy because mindfulness enables us to pay attention more, focus more and be present.

What you don't say

Being more aware of your body language plays a key part in face-to-face communication. It's often referred to as nonverbal communication and means anything other than words that communicates a message. So, everything from the way you choose to stand, shrug your shoulders and carry tension in your body to your appearance and the way you shake hands all communicate ideas to others. For example, you may say about someone: 'She *said* she thought it was a good idea, but I got the feeling that she wasn't very happy with it.' How did you get this feeling, this message? Remember that what you are doing here is decoding a message and you will be interpreting things like facial expressions (perhaps there was a particular facial expression you noticed that seemed to imply that despite what was said, she did not like the idea). It may have been something in her tone of voice which did not sound very enthusiastic – in other words, something did not seem to fit with what was being said verbally.

All of these things which we take into account when decoding a message and interpreting what someone is saying, over and above actual words, are referred to as 'metacommunication'. 'Meta' is from the Greek and means 'beyond' or 'in addition to'. Everything in the above example is about metacommunication.

However, if the impression was gleaned from voice inflection then this is what is known as '*paralanguage*', which conveys the opposite of the words themselves. When this happens we are more likely to pick up the meaning of paralanguage than the actual meaning of the language being used.

For example, if you were being sarcastic you might comment on something someone else has done by saying 'Thank you very much', in a tone with a particular emphasis on the 'very much', perhaps, that leaves the other person in no doubt that what you mean is just the opposite.

Similarly, using gestures and other facial expressions or body movements like shrugging your shoulders to indicate 'I don't know' or 'Don't ask me', or storming out of a room (indicating anger) communicate every bit as effectively as words may have done.

The important thing to remember here is that nonverbal communication is often interpreted subconsciously – nonverbal channels are the ones which we seem to be *least* aware of in ourselves, but *most* aware of in others.

Equally, silence is also a powerful communication tool. Have you ever been 'cut dead' by someone? How did you feel? The speech or lecture is finished and the speaker asks for questions – how do you feel about the silence? When someone asks us a question and we fail to answer we are still communicating something. When a speaker reaches the end of their talk, invites questions and there is total silence, the audience is also communicating. It's then difficult for that speaker to interpret the silence correctly – boredom? Disagreement? Rejection? Total satisfaction? Without any clearer feedback the silence is ambiguous and the speaker is left to guess the meaning – perhaps wrongly.

We are social creatures and our society is made up of responses to each other so feeling validated, acknowledged and reassured is important. Silence can be useful sometimes too – when it comes to listening or encouraging feedback.

Try this

When you next watch TV or overhear a conversation in a bus or train, see if you can observe how nonverbal communication is being used. Or try watching TV with the sound off and see if you can pinpoint nonverbal cues. Then start trying to be more aware of how you are using nonverbal communication.

In recent years there has been more and more interest in body language and researchers have tried to establish the exact nature of the relationship between this kind of nonverbal communication and the effect it has on the receiver. Anyone looking to improve communication skills needs to be sensitive to the human relations aspects in the communication process – and these aspects are often vividly revealed in body language!

Exercise: reading body language

1. How do you know that someone agrees with you, when you are speaking to them?

_____

_____

2. Can you tell whether someone has understood you, from the way they look at you?

_____

_____

3. List five examples of body language and what message they each convey:

_____

_____

_____

_____

Thinking point

Your nonverbal messages tend to reveal the degree of presence of sincerity, conviction, honesty, ability and knowledge; they reveal, too, a lot about you and your attitudes and feelings about the message you're transmitting. The body language of the receiver also reveals a lot about them and their feelings but, more importantly, will tell you the extent to which the other person or the audience is accepting or not accepting your message. In other words, body language provides you with instant feedback if you pay attention to it. If you are insensitive to it or unable to interpret it or read it this impacts your communication effectiveness considerably.

It follows that to be a good reader of body language you need to sharpen your powers of observation and your ability to decode the messages; you need to be more aware of the presence of these messages and their possible meanings; to be constantly alert to the effect of your own body language on other people as well as alert to the feedback available so that you can adapt your approach as needed.

So what? How you can use the information in this chapter to improve your face-to-face communication

Communicating well in person is probably one of the very best assets you have and it makes sense to cultivate it and to use it well. Having a stronger understanding of how we communicate face-to-face both verbally and nonverbally will help you to come across more authentically and positively in your communications with others. Needless to say, like with most of communication, it begins with your self-awareness.

Communication is a question of personal credibility

Research suggests that formal, prepared presentations account for only 10% of the time we spend communicating verbally which means that 90% of communication at work is informal and often one-to-one: meetings, briefings, discussions, responding to queries and challenges, negotiations, interviews and explanations. All of these can take place both on- and offline. Here are eight ways to tap into your communication potential when you are put on the spot and need to think clearly and speak with conviction and impact:

1. Be clear about what you want to achieve
Ask yourself what you want to achieve between the time you start talking and the time you stop talking. What do you want the person or people you are addressing to think, feel, know or do?

2. Structure
Decide how you are going to structure what you want to say. Sharing the structure with whoever you are talking to means that you now both know the ground you are going to cover – so that neither of you gets lost. While this may not be necessary in informal conversations it is really helpful when it comes to interviews, meetings, negotiations and explanations.

3. The power of three
In structuring what you want to say, try using the power of threes – three key points, three perspectives, three levels of detail, three benefits, three concerns, three points in time. We – and our listeners – can handle three pieces of information. It might sometimes be two and sometimes four, but threes work beautifully.

4. Think about which words you use and how many
No one is impressed by fancy words. No one is impressed by technical jargon. No one is impressed when we say too much. Use simple language that shows that you are responding to what you are being asked – not trying to impress someone else.

5. Listen
Verbal communication isn't just about talking! You will find out far more by listening and asking appropriate questions – and listening again – than by simply talking.

Even when you are talking you should still be listening hard for the response you are getting – so that you can ensure you are moving towards your objectives.

6. Use nonverbal communication too
What you say is only part of the story. How you say it – the intonation in your voice, your body language, how confident you look – are just as important; perhaps more so.

7. Check and double check
Check that you've been understood and check that you've achieved your objective – that you've given the other person what they wanted or needed – and had the impact you wanted or were aiming for.

8. Recap
To finish, a recap of your (three) key points will help to reinforce your messages.

Putting it into practice

The next chapter takes a closer look at three important areas of face-to-face communication that you are likely to encounter in the workplace:

Meetings – these will feature heavily in the workplace whether on- or offline. Unfortunately, many meetings are counterproductive – this section will give you insight into how to ensure clarity at a meeting, how to take part and contribute effectively, and how to stay present and communicate effectively.

Presentations and interviews – you will likely be attending a fair number of interviews in the near future and presentations are now part of any job role, whether formal or informal. Being able to present with confidence, credibility and clarity is a key skill to master.

Networking and conferences – many of your most successful opportunities will come from networking, both face-to-face and online, and conferences are a great way to continue professional development, make new contacts and source new ideas. It's important to know how to network well and authentically and how to create strong relationships which may well become your most important asset.

Further reading

Cuddy, Amy. 2016. *Presence: Bring your Boldest Self to your Biggest Challenges*. Orion.
Ekman, Paul. 2007. *Emotions Revealed, Second Edition: Recognizing Faces and Feelings to Improve Communication and Emotional Life*. Holt.
Farson, Richard and Rogers, Carl. 2015. *Active Listening*. Martino.
Goyder, Caroline. 2014. *Gravitas: Communicate with Confidence, Influence and Authority*. Vermillion.

Meetings, Presentations and Networking

What's in this chapter:

- Did you know? Key facts and statistics about meetings, presentations and networking
- Why meetings can often be a waste of time
- Tips for taking part in or leading effective meetings
- Why presentations will be a key feature of your working life
- Top tips for great presentations
- Top tips for great interviews
- The importance of networking and how to do it well

Did you know?

Key facts and statistics about meetings, presentations and networking

- Most meetings have no purpose or structure.
- Sometimes the best meetings are spontaneous and one-to-one.
- The fear of public speaking is known as 'glossophobia' and up to 75% of us suffer from some form of it (McClafferty, 2015).
- On average, every corporate job opening attracts 250 CVs but only four to six of these people will be called for an interview, and only one of those will be offered a job (GlassDoor, 2016).
- According to GlassDoor recruitment company, 79% of job seekers use social media in their job search and this figure increases to 86% of younger job seekers who are in the first 10 years of their careers (GlassDoor, 2016).
- Networking is likely to be one of the priorities when it comes to building relationships, getting work and being effective in the workplace.

Why meetings can often be a waste of time

Most meetings can be a waste of time and once you enter the workplace you will find that you probably do spend a fair bit of time in them! Even a weekly meeting will generate additional time caught up in preparation for the meeting, communication about the meeting and follow-up actions from the meeting. Even companies themselves acknowledge that their meetings, for the most part, are ineffective.

However, meetings as a form of communication are probably set to continue in most companies. This is because more and more companies are team-based companies and in team-based companies most work gets done in meetings.

A variety of tools and techniques (plus a healthy dose of common sense) can make meetings less painful, more productive, maybe even fun. What's important is that once you get into the workplace you have a good sense of how to contribute and communicate well within a meeting setting. When you first enter the workplace, some of your thinking and energy will be spent working out how you fit in with the organisation and company culture and meetings can help you to do that. However, it can also be tempting to wait until you have worked this out before you start contributing to meetings. By understanding more deeply what is happening in a meeting and how it is being managed you can use meetings to your advantage.

Meeting formats vary widely from company to company. Whether large or small, person-to-person, in a conference room or via web-based chat rooms, meetings can be efficient communication tools when thoughtfully conceived and well-managed.

Unfortunately, sometimes it can seem that people simply do not take work meetings seriously. They may arrive late, leave early and may spend most of their time doodling or checking their phones. This needn't and shouldn't be you. Meetings can be really productive if there is a clear agenda, a clear sense of collaboration and someone responsible for facilitating the meeting, minuting it and following it up. Meetings should be considered as work rather than something additional to work, as in 'meeting's over, let's get back to work'.

These are three specific meeting rules that seem to be universal:

1) **All meetings must have a stated purpose or agenda.** Without an agenda, meetings can easily turn into aimless social gatherings rather than productive working sessions.
2) **Attendees should walk away with concrete next steps or action items.** From Apple to the Toastmasters, the world's most successful organisations demand that attendees leave meetings with actionable tasks.
3) **The meeting should have an end time.** Constraints breed creativity. Not placing an end time can encourage rambling, and off-topic and trivial conversation.

Now, when you enter the workplace you may or may not have control over the meeting's purpose or agenda nor of how the meeting is facilitated, run and followed up. What you do have control over is your own actions and responses before the meeting takes place, during it and afterwards.

Meetings can provide you with several opportunities:

- Benefiting from the knowledge and opinions of others.
- Gaining maximum information from the backgrounds and experiences of your colleagues.
- Feeling a part of a policy or decision under which you will be working.
- Developing a better understanding and appreciation of your colleagues and the teamwork that can be developed among you.
- Expressing and communicating your thoughts to others.
- Evaluating your own opinions, beliefs and attitudes in the light of other people's.

One key aspect of meetings that you do have complete control over is your own preparation. This may require time and effort but will be very much worth your while – you will get far more out of the meeting and are likely to have far more to contribute, too. Your participation depends on how good a communicator you are.

Top tips for good meeting behaviour

Whatever anyone else may be doing, make sure you do these:

Come to the meeting. If you're scheduled to go to a meeting, make every attempt to get there. Being too busy is not really an option and will create a negative impression. When you do show up, be on time. Get there five minutes early if possible. If you're late, don't make excuses. Just apologise and sit down. Remember that people use excuses to make themselves feel better. If you are habitually late, work out why, and fix it. Whatever you do, don't waste the group's time by having them 'catch you up'.

Come prepared. If you are on the agenda to update or present or need to read or prepare something for the meeting, do it and do it to the very best of your ability.

Don't use your phone, email or text. It may not feel like it, but everything can wait. Put your phone away so you are not tempted to look at it. When you check your phone during the meeting, you give the impression to the speaker that you are not interested in what they have to say. Remember from the chapters about working smarter and avoiding distraction that not using your phone is easier said than done but will pay dividends as you will be concentrating on what is happening right in front of you. If others are using their phones (which is likely), simply ignore it.

Participate. If you don't usually like talking in meetings, you may have to force yourself once you are in the workplace. If you tend to be quiet, you may find that actually you are able to get to the point quickly and have a lot to add. Be ready to get involved on the spur of the moment because group interest in your contribution will be strongest at the beginning. However, do not talk just to talk. Before you say something in a meeting ask yourself if what you have to say adds value to the conversation. If not, don't say it.

Use the 'one-minute rule'. Try to talk at a number of points in the meeting rather than just saying everything that's on your mind at once. Unless you are presenting or setting up the discussion, once you talk more than a minute it's too long. If you tend to be a long talker, start timing yourself. A tip to stop someone from going on and on is to stare at their forehead. Strange but it works!

Don't take the group on meaningless tangents. Sometimes great new ideas emerge during a discussion that had nothing to do with the agenda item. That's good and to be encouraged. Try to avoid getting into a discussion topic that is completely off-track, like the results of a recent TV reality show.

Listen to others. Don't be the person who sits on the edge of their seat just waiting for an opening to say what they want to say. Meetings are a key time to use the active listening skills outlined in Chapter 5. Don't cut people off. Sometimes you need to do this in order to get into the conversation, but try to let the other person finish their thought first and find a good moment to jump in.

Watch your nonverbal body language. You know now that most of our communication comes from the way we use our bodies and face. Avoid making faces, rolling your eyes, crossing your arms, slouching in your chair, unless you want to send the message that you are extremely disinterested. Instead use positive body language by having an open stance, eye contact and leaning towards people.

Don't check out. If the topic doesn't interest you or is not important to what you do, it is still really important to pay attention and listen. Don't give in to any negative feelings or thoughts by expressing them. That means resisting any desire to make snide comments, be sarcastic or pointing. Whatever you may be feeling inside it is crucial that you are aware and choose the appropriate responses.

Recognise people. If you like what someone said or did, tell them. Everyone loves getting recognised in front of their peers and it's an important element of the A in autonomy and the R in the relatedness components of the SCARF model. See Chapter 1 – *Your Amazing Brain* for more on SCARF.

Ask probing and engaging questions. Many people tend to make one statement after the other at a meeting. If you want the team to consider your idea, try using a question rather than a statement and see what happens when you do. Assist the facilitator by helping to stay on agenda, watching the time, and letting others speak.

Make it fun. It's OK to laugh in a meeting but don't have side conversations, however tempting. This is really tough on the meeting facilitator.

Avoid suggesting new work for other people. If it's your idea, you own it.

Speak up when you disagree. Speak clearly and non-emotionally. It's not OK to keep quiet and then complain afterwards about a decision made at the meeting.

If you have to leave early, let people know up front. Then leave quietly.

Let the meeting end. Try not to bring up something at the very end of the meeting. If something does occur to you at the end it can be communicated via a follow-up discussion or perhaps included in one of the action points.

Follow through with action steps. Write actions down if you have been tasked to do something; do them; and then be prepared to present on what happened.

These are simple meeting rules to follow largely by being appropriately prepared before the meeting, being present and aware during the meeting and being accountable by carrying out follow-up actions after the meeting. Whether you are facilitating the meeting yourself or are a participant, the same rules apply.

Self-check

Think about being a participant at a work meeting.

1. What sorts of things can you do to help you prepare for the meeting?

_____

_____

_____

_____

2. What are some ways that you can contribute positively to the meeting?

_____

_____

_____

_____

3. How can you benefit from meetings and other small group discussions?

_____

_____

_____

_____

Taking minutes

Perhaps you are expected to take minutes from a meeting. At the very least, it's important to get a copy of the meeting agenda and use it as a guide or outline for taking notes and preparing the minutes – with the order and numbering of items on the minutes matching those of the agenda.

In addition, the agenda and/or meeting notice also provides information that will need to be included in the minutes, such as the names of all the meeting attendees, including guests or speakers, documents that are sent out with the agenda or handed out in the meeting – copies (digital or hard copy) of handouts should be stored with the meeting minutes for future reference and for sharing with those who were unable to attend the meeting (and others as determined by the meeting's Chair).

Before you start taking notes, it's important to understand the type of information you need to record at the meeting. As noted earlier, your organisation may have required content and a specific format that you'll need to follow, but generally, meeting minutes usually include the following:

- Date and time of the meeting
- Names of the meeting participants and those unable to attend (e.g. 'regrets' or 'apologies')
- Acceptance or corrections/amendments to previous meeting minutes
- Decisions made about each agenda item, for example:
    - Actions taken or agreed to be taken
    - Next steps
    - Any other business (AOB)
    - Next meeting date and time

Tips that might help your note-taking

Create an outline – having an outline (or template) based on the agenda makes it easy for you to simply jot down notes, decisions, etc. under each item as you go along. If you are taking notes by hand, consider including space below each item on your outline for your handwritten notes, then print these out and use this to capture minutes.

Check off attendees as they enter the room – if you know the meeting attendees, you can check them off as they arrive; if not, have folks introduce themselves at the start of the meeting or circulate an attendance list so that they can check themselves off.

Record decisions or notes on action items in your outline as soon as they occur to be sure they are recorded accurately

Ask for clarification if necessary – for example, if the group moves on without making a decision or an obvious conclusion, ask for clarification of the decision and/or next steps involved.

Don't try to capture it all – you can't keep up if you try to write down the conversation verbatim, so be sure to simply (and clearly) write (or type) just the decisions, assignments, action steps, etc.

Record it – literally, if you are concerned about being able to keep up with note-taking, consider recording the meeting (e.g. on your smartphone, iPad, recording device, etc.) but be sure to let participants know they are being recorded. While you don't want to use the recording to create a word-for-word transcript of the meeting, the recording can come in handy if you need clarification.

Try this

You are in charge of organising a company-wide social event. You are about to call a meeting with the organising group to discuss arrangements for the event. In this meeting, which is about six weeks away, you'll have to decide on location, food, music/ entertainment, tables and chairs, decorations and admission fee. You might even look for corporate sponsors to help fund the event.

1) What needs to be handled in your meeting?

_____

_____

_____

2) What sorts of roles and responsibilities may need to be allocated?

_____

_____

_____

3) What preparation work should be done before the meeting in order for it to be effective?

_____

_____

_____

4) What could you do before the meeting to ensure everyone will come with ideas and enthusiasm?

_____

_____

_____

5) What should you do during the meeting to ensure that your actions are taken forward?

_____

_____

_____

6) After the meeting, what can you do to ensure that other group members follow up on their promises to complete certain tasks?

_____

_____

_____

Try this

Observe a project team meeting, study meeting or workplace meeting.

Overall, how well was this meeting executed? Take notes on what happened (and didn't happen) during and immediately after the meeting so that you can answer the following questions.

- What was the purpose of the meeting? How do you know this?
- Was the purpose or objective met? How do you know this?
- What were some specific things that were effective? Explain and cite examples.
- What made the meeting ineffective? Explain, citing specific examples.
- If you were to lead this meeting, what would you have done differently and why?

Presentations and interviews

According to a famous and widely cited survey most of us are more terrified of giving a presentation than we are of dying which does not really make any sense when you stop to analyse it! For most of us the fear of giving a presentation is very real, though. There are all sorts of tips and ideas and plenty of resources that will help you prepare for a presentation and it's important to make ample use of these.

Fear of public speaking often feels like it hits you out of nowhere no matter how much you have prepared beforehand. Most people, regardless of how many presentations they give, experience some of this fear to a degree so understanding better where it comes from and having strategies in place to help you will go a long way towards building your confidence and skills in presenting.

Presentations will be part of your working life

It's very likely that you will need presentation skills for a number of different reasons:

Types of presentation	When you might find yourself doing this
Talks, seminars and conferences	These are likely to be informal; you might be sharing information or expertise in a particular area.
Proposals and sales pitches	You might have to present a proposal if you are starting a new business or pitching for work as a freelancer. This is more likely to be a persuasive presentation so that someone will buy your product or service.
	Throughout our lives we are 'selling' ourselves to teachers, prospective mates, neighbours or colleagues. But in the business world, we are most often selling our products, services or ideas.
Meetings	You may have to give an update, report or explanation about something. This could be formal with slides and other visuals or an oral update – either way, it is still a presentation.

Interviews	Similar to sales pitches and proposals – here you are selling yourself to get that job. It's useful to remember that if you have been invited to interview then you very likely fulfil all the other criteria for the position in terms of qualifications and relevant experience or skills. So the interview part is about *you* as a person and whether or not you are a good fit for the job. No matter how well qualified and skilled, if you do not come across well at interview you won't get the job!

Try this ✏

Think about your own job or the industry you are hoping to enter. List below the different situations in which you might have to give a presentation:

_____

_____

_____

_____

_____

It can be helpful to understand what is happening in our brains when we have to give a presentation. There is a part of your brain that is naturally constantly scanning the environment, looking for threats to your survival. In prehistoric times, being part of a group was essential to our survival. So one of the threats to our survival was being excluded from a group – this also related to the R (relatedness) in the SCARF model and our innate need to feel a connection with others (Chapter 1). Standing out in some way, saying something offensive or stupid, or not performing to expectations are all perceived reasons for possible exclusion from a group.

Fast forward to now. You're standing in front of a group ready to open your mouth and this part of your brain identifies this as a threatening situation. If you say something 'stupid', something 'awful' might happen – or, in the prehistoric context, you might die! It's no longer true that you might die, but what is happening is that your survival system is being activated: fight, flight or freeze. When it comes to public speaking the most common reactions are flight or freeze:

> **Flight** – You avoid public speaking if at all possible. If you do have to speak, you speak as fast as you can so that you get through it as quickly as possible.
> **Freeze** – You feel stiff and artificial as you speak, your mind goes blank.

Do either of those sound familiar?

The area of your brain which regulates your emotions will make you feel nervous when you're reminded of a previous nerve-wracking experience. For example, if you had an experience at school where you felt humiliated in front of your classmates, or suffered an embarrassing mind-blank in an important presentation, those strong emotional memories may return when you least expect them to.

Try this

Most people revise the awfulness of their nerve-wracking experience from somewhere near 100% to somewhere near 0%. They would prefer to relive that nerve-wracking presentation experience rather than experience an injury. The idea of physical pain quickly helps put the presentation experience into perspective.

The reality is that most of the things that happen to us in presentations are not that bad. They're nothing compared to some of the other things that might happen to us in life like relationship break-ups, loss of a loved one, and serious health issues. The most serious consequences of a presentation going badly might be losing a possible contract or opportunity and although this would naturally be disappointing it is *not* catastrophic.

The conscious thinking part of your brain will produce patterns of thinking that contribute to your nervousness and you can help reduce this by exploring your patterns of thinking, such as the cognitive behaviour exercises in Chapter 1 – *Your Amazing Brain,* that help to raise awareness of, to question and to revise these patterns. One of the most common patterns of thinking that contribute to the fear of public speaking are demands that we create and assume ourselves.

Here is an example of how this might happen: A couple of years ago I was delivering a new training workshop for a company in Bangladesh. I knew that the CEO would be one of the participants. I felt myself get a little nervous as we were setting up. When he walked into the room I got hot and my heart started racing. Why would I react in this way? I appear to have a demand around CEOs and it goes something like this:

'CEOs are really important and I must have their approval' and 'This is a brand new workshop and it's important that the CEO likes it.'

My demanding thought made me nervous. What was the result? I started to speak too fast and some of the instructions I gave for one of the exercises were unclear even though I knew the material inside out and had run the exercise many times before with other groups.

Here are some common demands people have about presenting and public speaking:

'I must be interesting and engaging.'
'I mustn't leave anything out.'
'I mustn't waffle.'
'I mustn't show I'm nervous.'
'I've got to be able to answer every question.'

Try this

Can you identify and articulate any demands you may have about public speaking? You may identify with some of the ones listed in the main text. Write down your own demands about public speaking here:

_____

_____

_____

_____

_____

Now do the same thing for any demands you have about interviews:

_____

_____

_____

_____

_____

Now, these demands will make you nervous because you can't guarantee that the demand will be met. So what you need to be able to do is reduce their power and you do this by rationally analysing the truth and usefulness of these demands.

Really, what you are doing here is the same as for the cognitive behaviour exercises in Chapter 1. For example, with my CEO demand I can see that it's not essential that the CEO approves of me and that whether or not he approves or disapproves is not going to have an impact on my work because I feel confident in what I am doing.

It's important to remember, too, that any time you are called on to give a presentation or to attend an interview this situation is based on others having confidence in you and in your abilities already – quite often the only person you need to persuade when it comes to presentation nerves is you!

Aside from getting to grips with your nerves, what else can you be doing to give a confident and convincing presentation or interview? The key is always going to be in the preparation but perhaps it's useful to distinguish presentations (whether pitches, proposals, seminars, talks or other types of presenting) from interviews at this stage.

10 tips for effective presentations

1) **Connect with your audience.** It can be hard to feel relaxed and be yourself when you're nervous but the most important thing you can do is connect with your audience. You do this by caring about the subject, being honest with the

audience about why it's important to you and why it matters and by showing your enthusiasm. Your audience will connect with that almost instantly. It also helps you take the focus off yourself.

2) **Focus on your audience's needs.** It's easy to become very focused on what you are going to say but take time to think about what your audience is going to get out of your presentation. Why are they there? As you prepare, think about what the audience needs and wants to know rather than what you can tell them. Simply shifting your focus will have an immediate effect. In the same way, while you are delivering the presentation you need to remain focused and alert to the audience (use your understanding of empathy and body language and pay attention to audience response). Make it easy for the audience to understand what you are saying. It's easier to do this if you have the key bullet points of your message ready rather than learning and reciting something by heart, as doing this prevents you from being in the moment.

3) **Concentrate on your core message.** When you are planning your presentation think about the key message (or three key points) for your audience to take away and then focus on communicating just that key message very briefly. Try condensing it to 15 words to keep the core message focused and brief. If anything you are planning to say does not contribute to that core message, then don't say it.

4) **Smile and make eye contact with your audience.** It is really easy to forget to do this, especially if you are feeling nervous. So keep remembering that this is about them, not you. When you smile and make eye contact, you are building rapport, which helps the audience to connect with you and your subject. It also helps you to feel less nervous, because you are talking to individuals, not to a great mass of unknown people.

5) **Start strongly.** It is a good idea to script the very beginning of your presentation because it's crucial that at that point you are able to grab your audience's attention and hold it. Remember that they will make up their mind about you in the very first few seconds or minutes. Don't start by explaining who you are – try a story or an attention-grabbing (but interesting and relevant) image on a slide. If you've started strong you are well on your way as after that the audience will be on your side.

6) **Remember the 10–20–30 rule for slides.** According to Apple you should never have more than 10 slides at most, your presentation should not be any longer than 20 minutes and the font on your slides should not be smaller than 30 font. Slides should only be enhancing what you are presenting and they should have as little information on them as possible – wherever possible try to use images if you can. If you want to give people more information you can provide a handout afterwards.

7) **Tell stories.** Stories are very powerful because we are hard-wired to respond to them. They help us to pay attention, and to remember things. If you can use stories in your presentation, your audience is more likely to engage and to remember your points afterwards. It is a good idea to start with a story, but there is a wider point too: you need your presentation to act like a story so try thinking about what story you are wanting to tell your audience and create your presentation to tell it.

8) **Use your voice.** The spoken word is actually a pretty inefficient means of communication, because it uses only one of your audience's five senses. That's why presenters tend to use visual aids, too. But you can help to make the spoken word better by using your voice effectively. Varying the speed at which you talk, and emphasising changes in pitch and tone, all help to make your voice more interesting and hold your audience's attention. For more about how to use your voice effectively see Chapter 8 about speaking on the telephone.

9) **Be aware of your body language.** As well as your tone of voice, your body language is crucial to getting your message across because it's one of the most important parts of communication and how messages are interpreted. Make sure that you are giving the right messages: body language to avoid includes crossed arms, hands held behind your back or in your pockets, and pacing the stage. Try to use open, confident gestures and move naturally – this is where rehearsal helps as your muscle memory is stronger than you think.

10) **Remember to breathe.** If you find presenting difficult, it can be hard to be calm and relaxed about doing it. One option is to start by concentrating on your breathing. Slow it down, and make sure that you're breathing fully. Make sure that you continue to pause for breath occasionally during your presentation too. Breathing will also move oxygen around your body, helping you to relax. Drinking water will help, too, to keep you hydrated.

Try this 🖍

Think of an upcoming opportunity to present. List some of the things you can do to help yourself:

Prepare your presentation:

_____

_____

_____

_____

During your presentation:

_____

_____

_____

10 tips for interviews

1) **Be ready to talk about what's on your CV.** You would not be at the interview without an excellent CV so it is important that you are able to discuss everything on it with confidence. Spend some time the day before reviewing it and getting prepared to talk about your employment history, education and personal interests

and experiences. Think about how all of these elements and your overall attitude could benefit the organisation – relate everything on your CV to what you can bring to the job. Do this by having your CV and the job description side-by-side and looking for ways to link them. Just going over this the day before will enhance the probability of you being able to draw on it during the interview.

2) **Do your research.** Probably the single worst thing you can do in a job interview is to go in without doing your research. To be taken seriously as a professional you need to know what the company does, who its main competitors are, and what some current challenges are. You can find a lot of this information on the company website, but you should also search for company news and performance on Google and in industry publications. If the company has a presence on Twitter, Facebook, LinkedIn or YouTube, familiarise yourself with their approach and be armed with your own opinions. Carrying out this level of research will also help you to understand where your role fits in, and will form the basis of your own questions at the end of the interview. It may also help you decide on the best clothes to wear for your interview.

3) **Talk confidently about how you can add value.** The company is potentially investing in you so try to show your interviewer what you can deliver beyond the basic job description. Try the STAR technique (situation, task, action, result) – this is a useful approach to help illustrate your accomplishments. Whatever skill you highlight, try to relate it to how you can add value in the job you're applying for, and what qualities you can bring to the company.

4) **Be prepared to answer standard competency-based questions.** It's impossible to predict what you're going to be asked in any given interview, and while there will be questions that are tailored to the job you're interviewing for, you'll be expected to tackle competency-based questions.

    Competency-based questions are useful for employers because your response acts as a good indication of how you approach certain situations, so preparing for the most common ones makes sense for any interview you are attending. How would you answer these questions?

- How do you prioritise your workload?
- Give me an example of a time you felt out of your depth. How did you handle this?
- Tell me about a time you've worked under a lot of pressure. What was the outcome?
- Give me an example of when you've had to persuade people that your idea was the best approach.
- Tell me about a risk you've taken in your professional life. How did you handle the challenge?

The more at ease you can become about answering these kinds of questions the easier it will be.

5) **Prepare your own questions in advance.** This is an important, but often overlooked, part of an interview. It's very likely you'll be given the opportunity to ask your own questions at the end of any job interview, and whether you think everything has been covered or not it doesn't look good if

you don't have anything prepared. You could ask about the company's vision and values, training and development opportunities, and how your role might progress over the coming years. This shows you're interested in a future with the business and care about where they're heading; it'll also give you the information you need to decide whether the role is right for you.

6) **Expect the unexpected.** Your reaction to unexpected questions can be a good reflection of your personality, your ability to think on your feet, and how you handle pressure – but try not to rush your answers as that could turn 'pressure' into 'panic'. It's perfectly acceptable to take your time to think about the question, and to ask your interviewer to clarify things if you're not sure what they're asking. Remember: if they've invited you for interview, they've seen something in you they like, so try to stay confident and keep your cool.

7) **First impressions are everything!** You only get one chance to make that first impression so make it count. You know already that what you'll be judged on within the first few minutes of meeting your interviewer will be nonverbal – from your appearance to your body language. So make sure you dress smartly and appropriately for the company. Greet your interviewer with confidence and enthusiasm, sit upright and lean slightly forward to indicate interest, and try to establish eye contact to build rapport.

8) **Keep communication clear and precise.** Interviews are two-way. When answering questions (or asking any of your own), make sure your tone is clear and precise, listen carefully to what's being asked of you, and take your time with your response. Remember to listen.

9) **Practice makes perfect.** Practice also boosts your confidence, lessens your nerves, and increases your chances of success. As with any skill, the more you practise your interview technique, the more you'll grow and develop. While you might not have endless interviews lined up to perfect your approach, you can try explaining your role to a friend; outline how you navigated a challenge at work, highlight your key achievements (backed up with facts and figures where possible).

10) **Check details.** All the preparation in the world won't get you far if you miss the main event, so before the day of your interview, check:
   • The time of the interview
   • The location and how you get there (print off a map if need be)
   • The times of public transport if you're relying on it to get you there
   • The name and job title of the person you're meeting.

See Chapter 11 – *Putting it All Together* for a more in-depth look at interviews.

Try this ✏

Think of an interview that is coming up. Based on the concepts and ideas outlined in this chapter and what you now know about the communication process, list here what you will do to help you prepare for the interview using these headings to help you:

Before the interview

Company research:

_____

_____

_____

Linking my CV to the job description:

_____

_____

_____

My journey on the day:

_____

_____

_____

My appearance:

_____

_____

_____

My expectations and demands around this interview:

_____

_____

_____

_____

What questions do I want to ask?

_____

_____

_____

During the interview

My listening skills:

_____

_____

_____

_____

My body language:

_____

_____

_____

My breathing:

_____

_____

_____

Networking

Networking is one of those areas that, like presentations, can be scary. It also conjures up someone 'working the room', making connections, being able to succinctly sum up what they do and doling out business cards. But natural networking is really much more about developing real relationships with people and building something that is mutually beneficial. So, looking at networking from the perspective of what you can give to others is a very good place to begin.

These days, if you hear the term 'networking', your mind may immediately jump to 'social networking' – and indeed, technology tools such as Facebook, Twitter and LinkedIn provide a powerful and convenient means of developing and maintaining your personal and professional connections and should definitely be used. There are more tips and ideas for building your social media network in the next chapter.

But there's more to a network than the number of people who 'friend' you on Facebook or follow you on Twitter or Instagram. On a deeper level, effective networking involves developing real relationships with other people, sharing relevant information and resources, and providing mutual support and encouragement on the path to reaching your goals. Your network can also open doors to potential career opportunities, and may even help you land a job.

Self-check

What are some of the reasons you might network?

Some of the reasons you might network:

- Sharing your knowledge and influence to help others.
- Uncovering unadvertised job opportunities.
- Obtaining referrals.
- Gaining interview practice.
- Learning more about a position, organisation and industry.
- Making new contacts.

Networking can happen anywhere where there is an opportunity to create that connection. Yes, it does happen at conferencing, networking and breakfast events but it can just as easily happen at an informal gathering, during a long train journey or a chance conversation over a post on LinkedIn. Networking happens both in person and online. You will be using the same skills that you need for any personal encounter in terms of empathy and being present so make those your cornerstones and you won't go far wrong.

Try this

You are connected to a far wider network than you think!

Think of a current goal you are pursuing – write it down here:

Brainstorm a list of all the people who are somehow connected to this goal and may be able to help you – don't discount any connection or possible contact.

What are some of the ways you might begin to reach out to these people?

Networking at conferences and events

I recently returned from a conference in India and another event in Bangladesh where there were great networking opportunities. At both I couldn't help but notice the proliferation of business card exchange that was going on. I found myself joining in and doling out my own card as well as adding loads to the now very large stash sitting on my desk. Truth is, I'm actually fairly unlikely to do anything with these contacts and they will join the others I've collected over the years. Yet we still engage in this mindless exchange of business cards.

There is a pattern to networking successfully and this is the same whether it's a networking event or an opportunity such as work experience placements or nurturing introductory contacts into a company. It is this: it's definitely not enough to have a brief conversation and exchange contact details or even to 'follow up' contacts and introductions with a friendly email. Instead, there has to be a strong reason to connect and to engage. That is only going to happen if you create a real spark with someone. That spark may well have nothing to do with work or even how you have met. It may have nothing to do with what you can offer them or potential areas you might work in together. It has everything to do with you as a person, your warmth, your personality, your ability to chat and make conversation, precisely without an agenda.

Networking has changed and yet we need to build our networks now more than ever. We live in an environment of constant information exchange. If that information is not worthwhile to us in that moment, it is irrelevant. Think about how much information you're bombarded with each and every day, how many emails, likes and shares – chances are you delete most of this *unless* it is meaningful or has come about through a relationship you trust and respect. Everything is about people and nurturing relationships. That will only happen by being yourself. Networking has become thoughtful and is all about engaging and learning and this equally applies to online networking too.

Most of the time at conferences and events people have their head in their smartphone or tablet – that alone makes it quite hard to create a spark or connection. It's equally hard when a conversation becomes transactional or ends up being purely an exchange about what the respective parties 'do' as in 'what do you do?'

What I've found when I've been to a networking event or conference, or even at a social occasion, is that the people I actually really connected with are those I've genuinely liked (in person, not on social media!). Those I've shared some fun conversation with as well as meaningful talk where we've discussed interesting aspects of our work. Those where we've discussed things that are important to each of us, things that we are passionate about. The connection or follow-up after this will tend to be via Twitter or LinkedIn and from that opportunities are free to arise naturally and organically.

Networking today requires us to bring and be our best selves, to know ourselves and to be able to connect with others with an easy confidence and without an agenda. To share, engage and learn.

Try this ✎

Think about your own network – this will include friends, family, university contacts, work contacts and work experience contacts.
  Use this table to categorise and list them:

Type of contact	Description
Operational	These are people who can help you get your work done. They will often be internal (i.e. university or workplace) and current.
Personal	These are people who can help you grow personally and professionally. They are usually external and share common interests.
Strategic	These are people who can help you shape your future goals and direction. They may be internal or external to your organisation and are future oriented.

Ideally you need an even balance across these types. Can you identify where you might need to grow your network?

Are you an introvert or an extrovert?

If you are an introvert you:	If you are an extrovert you:
Think, then speak	Speak, then think
Prefer small groups	Enjoy being in bigger groups
Are comfortable being alone	Have lots of friends
Know a few people well	Get your energy from other people
Take risks (carefully!)	Dive into new situations with energy
Prefer solitude as a catalyst for creativity	Thrive on surprises and unpredictability
Focus on one thing at a time	Are a good multitasker

At first glance it may seem that it is easier for extroverts to network – but not necessarily!

If you are an introvert here's what to focus on. The same applies to extroverts, of course, too.

- It's not about selling yourself. It's about helping other people.
- It's not about becoming popular but about learning and sharing.
- If it's hard to talk to strangers, make it easy for them to talk to you.
- Ask open questions.
- Be more interested in them than in yourself.
- Look for ways to help them.
- Follow up meetings with ideas, offers to help or recommendations.
- Make it easy for others to find you (using online platforms such as Twitter and LinkedIn).

Further reading

Gallo, Carmine. 2014. *Talk Like TED: The 9 Public Speaking Secrets of the World's Top Minds*. Macmillan.

Ludovico, Emilia. 2016. *Business Networking Events: The Emotional Intelligence Skills You Need to Business Networking Successfully: Volume 3* (Emotional Intelligence Series). CreateSpace Independent Publishing Platform.

Reed, James. 2015. *Why You?: 101 Interview Questions You'll Never Fear Again*. Portfolio Penguin.

Smith, Richard. 2015. *Interview Skills, Techniques and Questions, Resume and CV Writing – HOW TO GET HIRED: The Step-by-Step System: Standing Out from the Crowd and Nailing the Job You Want*. CreateSpace Independent Publishing Platform.

Getting Social Media Right

What's in this chapter:

- Did you know? Facts and statistics about social media
- Types of social media platforms
- How social media is changing the way we communicate and how we work
- Tips for leveraging social media in finding work
- Getting your LinkedIn profile right
- Instant messaging – is it the new email?
- Mindful ways to use social media
- So what? How you can use the information in this chapter to get social media right

Did you know?

Facts and statistics about social media

- More people own a mobile device than a toothbrush.
- The number of people who use Facebook is probably bigger than the largest country on earth.
- Grandparents are the fastest growing group of users on Twitter.
- On Instagram there are three times more likes for infographics than for any other type of content.
- YouTube – by 2018 video will take over mobile usage.
- You're more likely now to 'YouTube it' than 'Google it' meaning that internet users are rapidly moving towards video content and imagery over reading.

And did you know that:

- Twitter works as a stress ball, increasing the levels of oxytocin, a hormone known for its soothing and calming effects.
- Each time we receive a notification, a particular area in our brain is activated, giving us the same sense of satisfaction and pleasure we experience from eating, making love and earning money. Wow! But we

also know it causes us to be distracted (see Chapter 2 – *How to Overcome Distraction*).

- Social media helps our body produce adrenaline, which speeds up the process of addiction. People find it harder to quit social media than smoking!
- Five hours a day are enough to rearrange the way your brain operates. According to the 2016 Global Web Index report for social media usage, the average person has five social media accounts and spends around 1 hour and 40 minutes browsing these networks every day. This number is growing exponentially, with most of us being connected to social media most of the day. Our attention span is dropping as a result.

Types of social media platform

One of the challenges in writing a chapter about social media is the sheer pace of change in this area. It is hard to predict future trends because the way we use social media is changing all the time. Around the world, billions of us use social media every day, and that number is continuing to grow minute by minute.

According to a Statista 2016 survey it is estimated that by 2018, 2.44 billion people will be using social networks, up from 0.97 billion in 2010. That is a big increase – however, this number could easily be more.

What is social media?

It's not that we don't know what it is, as we use it all the time, but it is useful to have a working definition of social media:

According to the Merriam-Webster dictionary the definition of social media is:

forms of electronic communication through which users create online communities to share information, ideas, personal messages, and other content.

The popularity of social media sites has transcended languages, borders and cultures, and it is probably no exaggeration to say that we are witnessing a social media revolution.

We use it for every part of our lives – in our personal relationships, for entertainment, at work and in our studies. To put it into some context, according to the World Economic Forum (Guzman and Vis, 2016), every minute we collectively send more than 30 million messages on Facebook and almost 350,000 tweets.

Social media is everywhere and new platforms keep emerging all the time. Below is a list of the most common types of platform at the time of writing.

Self-check

Have a look at the list of social media types and note down in the third column which of these platforms you use most.

Types of social media platform	How it's used	Which do I use most?
Social networking sites	These are typically sites such as Facebook, Google Plus and LinkedIn where profiles and information can be shared as well as updates, articles, news and comments.	
Micro-blogging sites	The most well-known one is Twitter but also sites like Tumblr and Friend Feed with new ones cropping up all the time. These are sites where you can post short content to followers that then might lead to a link to your website or to another social media profile. Many companies now have Twitter handles, allowing them to post information and news and also allowing consumers to give feedback (positive or negative!) very quickly.	
Publishing tools	These will allow you to easily set up your own blog and even a website. The most well-known one is WordPress but there are many others.	
Collaboration tools	This is where you can collaboratively add to a body of information – the most popular is Wikipedia which has spawned smaller, more specialised sub-sites like WikiTravel and WikiBooks.	
Rating/review sites	There are lots of these and they enable you to give reviews about something you have purchased or visited. The most well-known ones are sites like Amazon and TripAdvisor but many others exist, allowing you to review and rate everything from movies to favourite food items.	
Photo sharing sites	These sites focus on images and photos (either taken yourself or gathered around the Web). The most well-known ones are Instagram, Pinterest, Snapchat and Flikr and you can add comment and titles to most of them.	

Video sharing sites	YouTube is fast becoming the most popular communication channel but there are others like Vimeo and Viddler. Snapchat is a fast growing hybrid which allows content to be posted and only seen for a few seconds before it disappears.
Personal broadcasting tools	These allow users to stream their own live content and are also a growth area. Examples are Blog Talk Radio and Livestream.
Virtual worlds	Popular in gaming and a huge innovation area. Examples include Second Life, World of Warcraft and FarmVille.
Location-based services	These are often connected to other social media platforms allowing you to post where you are in the world, i.e. Facebook Places, Foursquare, Check-ins and Yelp.
Widgets	Widgets allow you to add badges and 'like' buttons (usually linked to other social media sites such as Twitter and Facebook) to your blog or website.
Social bookmarking and curating platforms	These platforms bring together news articles and items of interest connected with themes and topics that you can select and save. There are lots of these platforms and typical examples are Digg, Delicious and Curator.
Group buying platforms	These platforms allow companies or small businesses to feature a discounted service or product to a mass audience. Once a critical mass is reached, buyers can take advantage of the offer. Examples include sites such as Groupon, Living Social and CrowdSavings.
Group chat applications	WhatsApp is a free-to-download messenger app for smartphones. WhatsApp uses the internet to send messages, images, audio or video. The service is very similar to text messaging services; however, because WhatsApp uses the internet to send messages, the cost of using WhatsApp is significantly less than texting. It is popular with teenagers because of features like group chatting, voice messages and location sharing.

As you can see, this list is a guide and serves more as an introduction to social media sites. It does not include applications (although I did include WhatsApp at the end) which add a whole new layer to being online. The arena is changing so fast that by the time you read this even more platforms will have emerged, others may have merged together and some may be obsolete. What is abundantly clear is that social media is and will continue to be a key part of how we communicate and a key part of our work.

How social media is changing the way we communicate and how we work

Our digital footprint

If you think about what this means in terms of your 'digital footprint' there are a number of areas to think about.

If you completed the exercise above to include which platforms you use the most it will reinforce just how much we use social media each and every day.

Every day, whether we want to or not, most of us contribute to a growing portrait of who we are online; a portrait that is probably more public than we assume.

This portrait helps companies target content at specific markets and consumers, helps employers look into your background, and helps advertisers track your movements across multiple websites. Whatever you do online, you might be leaving digital footprints behind.

So no matter what you do online it's important that you know what kind of trail you're leaving, and what the possible effects can be. Your digital footprint is all the stuff you leave behind as you use the internet. Comments on social media, Skype calls, app use and email records – it's part of your online history and can potentially be seen by other people, or tracked in a database.

Social media in the workplace

Smartphones, the internet, tweeting and blogging are all innovations that we have started to accept as part of our working lives, helping us to work more flexibly, stay in touch for longer and respond to each other quicker. As we can see from the chapters on working smart and avoiding distraction, these devices have both positive and negative impacts which means that many companies now have a social media policy that includes what is and what is not acceptable for general behaviour at work regarding use of the internet and social media sites.

Many businesses have been adept at harnessing the power of social media to their advantage. Others have been less so, but they are catching on. However, it is never plain sailing in the world of social media. As well as the benefits, social media throws up some huge challenges and real problems. It is now clear that employers and employees both need to consider how social media sites may affect employment.

Social media use has an impact on communications among managers, employees and job applicants, how organisations promote and control their reputation, and how colleagues treat one another. It can also distort what boundaries there are between home and work.

Many employers have been quick to use social media to recruit staff. Others have been flexible at allowing employees to use social media in the workplace to develop business and commercial relationships. Some employers have simply been keen to use social media as a better way of engaging with their staff and fostering a more collegiate environment. Because there is no clear standard of how to use social media at work it can result in employees misusing social media at or outside of work to the disadvantage of their employer. They may have used social media to post inappropriate comments about colleagues or their organisation. It is still a grey area with legislative questions too.

For example, is it lawful to vet job applicants using social media sites? What legal risks arise when permitting employees to use social media at work? How can an employer manage the risks that arise?

These are all questions companies are rapidly addressing through clear and transparent social media policies.

Social media is shaping the world we live in

Our growing love of social media is not just changing the way we communicate and the way we work – it's changing the way we do business, the way we are governed, and the way we live in society. And it's doing so at breakneck speed. Here are five observations and predictions for the way social media is changing the world from experts from the Global Agenda Council (World Economic Forum, 2016). All of these will impact how we use social media and how we communicate on social media platforms, at work as well as privately. The industry you find yourself working in is highly likely to be using social media as part of its strategy for marketing, doing business and targeting customers.

1. Across industries, social media is going from a 'nice to have' to an essential component of any business strategy

It started in the newsroom, as Claire Wardle of the Tow Center for Digital Journalism explains (Wardle, 2016): 'In just seven years, newsrooms have been completely disrupted by social media. Social media skills are no longer considered niche, and solely the responsibility of a small team in the newsroom. Instead social media affects the way the whole organisation runs.'

This trend has been spreading to businesses beyond the newsroom for some time now and will continue to do so. The social web and mobile technologies have accelerated the rate at which relationships develop, information is shared and influence takes hold. Businesses now use social media for digital marketing and customers use social media platforms to give feedback to businesses.

It also means that consumers have much bigger influence over business.

When Netflix announced it was changing its pricing structure, its customers revolted, posting 82,000 negative comments across its blogs and on Facebook and Twitter.

Within months the company lost 800,000 customers and two-thirds of its market value.

That's the speed of social – everything happens faster than ever before.

However, it is also an opportunity for businesses to stay closer to customers, connect to them and engage with them in entirely new ways.

The companies that will be successful in the future recognise the need for fundamentally changing the way they engage with their customers, and are transforming themselves into social enterprises and radically altering the way they manage their businesses.

A good example of how organisations can use social media to benefit their brand is KLM, one of the world's largest airlines. It uses social media to make connections with its customer base.

It engages customers on social networks where they can ask questions, check in for flights and have conversations about travel.

In one innovative campaign, KLM surprised passengers who had checked in on Twitter at the airport with a small personalised gift – something to enjoy on their trip.

The endeavour generated a phenomenal amount of good feeling that can translate into customer loyalty and have a powerful ripple effect: the KLM Twitter feed was viewed more than one million times during the month of the campaign.

2. Social media platforms may be the banks of the future

Imagine being able to pay your rent or make an investment through your favourite social network. That might not be too far off. According to Richard Eldridge of Lenddo (Eldridge, 2016):

> Social media is transforming banking relationships in very significant ways, from improving customer service to allowing users to send money to others via online platforms. New financial technology companies are using social media to help people simply open a bank account. Social media can even impact your ability to get a loan.

There will undoubtedly be challenges to overcome such as maintaining standards of security and implementing more sophisticated social media policies. These are issues which may well have been addressed by the time you read this book.

3. Social media is shaking up healthcare and public health

The health industry is already using social media to change how it works, whether through public health campaigns or virtual doctor's visits on Skype. It has also helped groups of people, such as patients suffering from the same condition, stay in touch. According to Shannon Dosemagen of Public Laboratory for Open Technology and Science and Lee Asae of Mayo Clinic Center for Social Media and its Social Media Health Network, 'social media has been responsible for relevant changes in both personal and community health, especially by making it easier for large numbers of people to rapidly share information' (Asae and Dosemagen, 2016).

Although this sharing of information can be very positive and helps official agencies and experts, it also allows non-experts to share information perhaps even more rapidly and it is this kind of sharing that the health industry will need to plan for in order to respond to and counter any misinformation, as well as to support accurate information, using social media to do so.

4. Social media is changing how we govern and are governed

Civic participation and engagement has been transformed with social media: social media allows citizens to be the source of ideas, plans and initiatives in an easier way than ever before, according to Eileen Guo of Impassion Media (Guo, 2016). In the future, we can expect more and more leaders to embrace this type of transparent governance, as it becomes easier for them to interact with their constituents. It is much easier now to interact through online town halls and for people to have direct input on government initiatives via online platforms.

This is a very different kind of relationship than before social media, where governments were typically the gatekeepers of information, and it calls for a complete rethink of the concept of governance as power shifts become stronger.

5. Social media is helping us better respond to disasters

From Facebook's Safety Check (Chaykowski, 2016), which allows users in disaster zones to mark themselves as safe – to the rise of the CrisisMappers Network (CDAC Network, 2016) we can see many examples of how social media and digital communications more broadly are helping people respond to disasters.

That looks set to continue. In fact, more and more of us will be using social media to contribute to disaster relief from wherever we are:

> Digital responders can immediately log on when news breaks about a natural disaster or human-created catastrophe. Individuals and teams are activated based on skill sets of volunteer and technical communities. These digital responders use their time and technical skills, as well as their personal networks in an attempt to help mitigate information overload for formal humanitarian aid in the field. (Leson, 2016)

These digital humanitarians will help close the gap in worldwide disaster response.

And there are more changes – in fact, the one thing we can be 100% certain of is that social media will continue to change and all of these changes will impact how we use it and how we communicate.

Emerging changes

Below are some areas which are rapidly changing and evolving:

Live streaming – this is already very popular and only set to get bigger. Companies will use live streaming to broadcast live business activities including conferences, interviews, customer support, product demonstrations and special offers.

On-platform content – instead of using webpages for publishing articles it is going to be far more likely that companies will start pushing articles directly to

Facebook, ensuring a much faster upload and much stronger visibility. Many businesses will be forced to compare the benefits of showing content on Facebook with the advantages of bringing users to their webpages.

Snapchat – this has the exact opposite effect of slow-burn content like a good YouTube video or a well-written blog post. Snapchat means you create carefully crafted content that disappears as soon as it's online. Yet many large companies are on board and are keen to interact with Snapchat's young audience – you are probably very familiar with this platform already. They'll be relying on you to churn out valuable but disposable content.

The huge rise in use of video – between April and November 2015, Facebook doubled average daily video views from four billion to eight billion (Griffith, 2016). Those figures are only going to grow. Facebook has already made it clear that it prefers video content to link posts and even images, so to build any kind of successful social media campaign you will need to pull out a video camera and get shooting!

Virtual reality – just as video is a more engaging form of content than still imagery, so virtual reality will be the next and most engaging step forward for content.

All of the ways we use social media and continue to use these platforms are a part of how we communicate and they will all rapidly be, if they are not already, part of the workplace you are in. Understanding how to use these platforms beyond how you might be using them now is going to be crucial. You may only be using social media for your private use but actually you probably also use it as a consumer and soon you'll likely be using it in some way at work or even helping the company you work for use it more effectively.

Managing social media effectively

One of the main facets of all of these changes is the immediacy of this type of communication. We already know that because of this we need to be more aware of how our messages come across to others and ensuring that our online communications are well thought through, but at the same time this can seem counter-intuitive because of the amount of information being pushed out requiring on-the-spot responses. At work you may be on the receiving end of, as well as being responsible for sending out, multiple streams and sources of information, which means becoming even better at filtering out what is not relevant and ever-more discerning about what information to actually focus on, whether receiving or sending it. If much of our mass and immediate communication is now going to be online, a strong awareness of this is more important than ever.

There are lots of helpful services around for managing social media accounts, both professionally and personally, but far less guidance on how we should best communicate using these tools. We need structure and discipline to communicate effectively via these means and that has to come from ourselves. At this point it is useful to remember Chapter 4 on managing email and Chapter 3 on working smarter. We can engage with social media in a thoughtful and positive way the more aware we are of how and when to best use it and the more we understand about its impact on our communication skills.

Using social media for job hunting

Social media is also going to be important for you when it comes to looking for work. Ninety-two per cent of companies now use social media platforms for recruitment – you can use this to your advantage by being savvy about how you interact with these companies as well as nurturing and looking after your own social media profiles.

Tips for leveraging social media in your job searches

Social media can be a great tool for finding work and indeed most companies use social media platforms to recruit so you may already be quite knowledgeable about what is out there if you've already started job hunting. It's likely that you already use social media a lot personally but it's very important to know how to use it effectively for professional purposes:

1. Clean up your profiles

This may seem very obvious and hopefully you are aware of this already. It is important that any public information on your various profiles is super clean. This doesn't just mean personal information and photos of social events – you should also consider removing articles that could be perceived as being politically divisive or could be considered offensive, posts that are random or that may come across as self-indulgent or long rants on a certain topic, and the like. There are tools that can help you search your feeds for things to delete so these are worth exploring.

2. Be selective about your social media accounts

Being 'active on social media' doesn't mean opening an account on every platform possible. Quite the opposite in fact! It's much better to have a well-crafted, up-to-date account on one or two platforms than to have a number of different accounts that are rarely used. Professionally, you should have a LinkedIn account, and Twitter at the least. Beyond that, consider what's really important for your industry. If you are in marketing, for example, there will be certain social media platforms that will be highly relevant to use. It is up to you to research and discover the ones that make most sense for you.

3. Use your real name

It can be tempting to pick a punchy nickname or handle when making your profiles but, as much as possible, always use your real name. This looks more professional and means that people will be able to find your profiles when they search for your name. If you have a common name or often go by a nickname, try to choose a consistent name that you can use across platforms, and try to have your real name somewhere on each account.

4. Keep your image professional and consistent

You should have a clear, friendly, recent and appropriately professional image to use across all platforms. If you are not sure what 'appropriately professional' means, take a look around at what the people in your industry are wearing to see how competent, influential and friendly your photo makes you look.

5. Get your personal branding right

In addition to a consistent name and consistent photo, you should have a consistent 'brand' across your social platforms. You want people to know who you are, what you do and where you're going. Make sure your messages are consistent across all platforms that you are using. It should be clear what you do, what industry you work in and the types of role you have had or are considering. This may well be the first point at which potential employers decide whether or not to engage with you.

6. Use your social accounts as jumping off points

A social media account should never live in isolation – it should link to somewhere that people can learn more about you. On all your social media accounts, make sure to include a link to the projects you're working on from current jobs or past jobs, your personal website, your blog, or anywhere else someone could learn more about you. It is important to have a consistent and clear online image.

7. Bring all your accounts together in one place

Conversely, make sure there's a central hub where you can collect all of your various presences around the web. A personal website or landing page is a great option, or you could simply make sure to link to them all from your LinkedIn profile. Doing this will mean that whenever potential recruiters or contacts search for you on social media for work opportunities, they can easily find all the profiles you want them to see.

8. Then make sure you put them on your job search materials

Your social media profiles can be a great representation of who you are and where you're going, so make sure they're out there! Put your Twitter handle on your CV, mention your industry-specific network in your cover letter, and tell people where to find you on your business card or your email signature. If you've done the work to make your social media profiles good and professional, don't be shy about sharing them!

9. Don't use social media for professional communications

While it's okay to promote your professional social media profiles in your materials when searching for jobs, don't use them for job-search related communications. In other words, you shouldn't be badgering companies you're applying to on Facebook or following up with recruiters after an interview on Twitter. In these circumstances a well-placed email or phone call may be a better approach after a period of time.

10. Use scheduling tools to stay on top of things

Make sure that you are current and visible. There are plenty of tools out there that will allow you to schedule, get ahead, share things directly from your browser, and hardly have to think about keeping an active social presence. Try to make use of one of these tools – most are free – to streamline your social media presence.

Try this ✐

Take a morning or afternoon to carefully review the social media profiles and platforms that you currently use, from a professional perspective:

Are there any that you could stop using? Any that you should start using?

Would you be happy for a potential employer to view your social media profiles? Why? Why not?

Is your LinkedIn profile up to date? Do you have a LinkedIn profile? If not, now may be the best time to create one!

Are your platforms consistent – do you have content that you could post on your LinkedIn site or even your website? If you do not have a website, do you need one and could now be a good time to set one up?

Getting your LinkedIn profile right

Because many recruiters and employers use LinkedIn and because many may well look at this before any CV is sent, it is worth taking the time to go through your LinkedIn profile now.

Activity/Task: Build a LinkedIn profile – use this activity to either create your LinkedIn profile or review the one that you currently have and revise it:

1) **Start with a professional photo.** If you don't have a professional headshot, add that to your to-do list, go with the cleanest, most professional looking snapshot you have – and upgrade as soon as possible. And smile! Remember: that photo may be your first impression with a potential employer.

2) **Make your headline stand out.** By default, LinkedIn populates your headline with your job title and current company if you're working. Consider listing your areas of expertise and speaking directly to your audience. If you want your profile to be searchable, include important keywords. Try to keep your headline to about 10 words.

3) **Fill out the 'summary' field with five or six of your main achievements.** Use bullets to make this easy to read. Think about your target reader and then paint a picture of how you can make that person's life easier. You can also add media files, including videos, so why not create a little introduction video? Be creative as it will help you stand out.

4) **Add images or documents to your experience.** Did you know that you can add media files to your experience? It's a great way to create a visual portfolio so if you have anything that you have written, designed, developed or created include it here, even more so if this is relevant to your industry in some way.

5) **Fill out as much of the profile as possible.** That includes skills, voluntary work, education, etc. There is a lot of room here to add interesting things that may not necessarily be on your CV, but paints you as a well-rounded individual. One quick tip: if your volunteer experience directly pertains to your job search,

put it in as work history, so it's up in the relevant section and not down at the bottom.

6) **Keep your work history relevant.** You don't need to list every single job you ever had. Instead, only list the jobs that are relevant to your current career goals. This becomes more important as your career evolves, of course.

7) **Add links to relevant sites.** If you have a work-related blog or online portfolio, make use of the three URLs you are allowed on your profile and link to it.

8) **Ask for recommendations.** Endorsements are great, but recommendations are the currency of the realm on LinkedIn. Reach out to past colleagues, lecturers, managers and associates and ask that they write you a recommendation.

9) **Use status updates to share industry-relevant content.** This can help show recruiters that you are focused and in-the-know in your industry.

Is instant messaging the new email?

With more communications platforms to choose from, people aren't using email as they once did. Today, there are too many real-time communications platforms to track. Along with email, people can chat through tweets, Gchat, Yik Yak, Snapchat, Facebook, Instagram, Viber, Skype, HipChat, FireChat, Cryptocat, and – perhaps most popular of all – text messaging. This kind of messaging is about having a shared digital space so that people can dip in and out of the conversation as needed.

According to an IBM survey of more than 1600 CEOs, 75% of them identified developing a more open and collaborative culture as being critical for managing the complexity of business today (IBM, 2010). The upcoming generation of workers (that's you) is not only among one of the most educated, it also favours transparent work tasks, expressiveness, and above all, a collaborative work environment. This inclination towards teamwork is influencing subtle changes in communication preferences. It is likely when you enter the workplace that, certainly internally, email may well not be the preferred form of communication. Depending on where you work and in which industry, of course, the preferred medium may well be a shared digital platform. It creates a more open exchange of ideas, and a more dynamic and flexible workplace culture.

Try this

- How often would you estimate you use online messaging and texting in the course of a day?
- What do you like about online messaging platforms?
- Do you like the idea of their use in the workplace? Why? Why not?

What drives your use of social media?

You probably use social media without a second thought, but as with all communication it is easy for messages to be misinterpreted in the speed of posting. It is worth knowing that every time we log on to social media we do so looking to fulfil our own psychological needs. These could be anything from acknowledgement to attention, approval, appreciation, acclaim, assurance or inclusion. Before you post, ask yourself: am I looking to be seen or validated? Is there something more constructive I could do to meet that need? Refer also to the chapters on managing distraction and working smarter (Chapters 2 and 3 respectively) to help you think about how you use digital platforms, whether for personal or professional use.

Try this

Consider these questions:

- How often do you post on social media?
- What are your reasons for posting?
- Are you aware of posts that seek acknowledgement, approval, appreciation, acclaim, assurance or inclusion? Have a look at your past 10 posts and check for yourself which of these categories you would put them in.
- Have you ever experienced social media communication problems – where a discussion has got out of control or where a post has led to a series of comments? What impact has this had on you, your friends, family and network?

So what? How you can use the information in this chapter to get social media right

You may or may not be well-versed in social media and you may already use it as part of your daily life. To what extent you currently use it professionally will depend on whether or not you are working. However, even before entering the workplace, having a good awareness of your digital footprint is important, as well as knowing how to leverage your understanding of social media to help you professionally too.

As with any other online communication tool, what is important is understanding how to use social media so that how you come across is unambiguous and clear. Your personal use of it will be different to your professional use of it. At the same time, social media profiles are visible to potential employers so you will need to think carefully about your online presence and whether or not your personal and professional profiles are aligned.

Many of the same principles for communicating via social media are similar to email in the sense of using empathy and clarity and thinking about what you post and why. The great thing about social media platforms is that they do provide an opportunity for you to build a personal online presence, for potential employers to get to know you before they decide to interview you and a fantastic opportunity for networking. Use them wisely and you may well find that most of your opportunities, creative ideas and new friendships and relationships come from these platforms more than anywhere else. Support these with a strong face-to-face presence (Chapter 5 – *Face-to-Face Communication*) and that is a powerful and rewarding combination!

Further reading

Boniface, Susie. 2016. *The Bluffer's Guide to Social Media*. Bluffers.

Casnocha, Ben and Hoffman, Reid. 2013. *The Start-up of You: Adapt to the Future, Invest in Yourself, and Transform Your Career*. Random House.

Fuchs, Christian. 2013. *Social Media: A Critical Introduction*. SAGE Publications.

Kawasaki, Guy. 2014. *The Art of Social Media: Power Tips for Power Users*. Portfolio Penguin.

Using the Telephone

What's in this chapter:

- Did you know? Facts and statistics about the telephone
- How we use telephone now and why this is changing
- Good reasons to make or receive a phone call
- The power of your voice
- The role of oxytocin
- Using power poses
- Basic phone rules
- When it can be good to make a phone call
- So what? How you can use the information in this chapter to boost your telephone skills

Did you know?

Facts and statistics about the telephone

- According to a Deloitte 2015 study on mobile consumers, most people own a smartphone but the number of people who use their phone to make voice calls is falling.
- The same study noted that the average smartphone owner spends more than two hours each day using the device. During that time, smartphone owners spend an average of 25 minutes using their phone to browse the web, 17 minutes on social networking, 13 minutes playing games and 16 minutes listening to music. Many also use their smartphone for photography or as an alarm clock.
- Making phone calls with the smartphone is only the fifth most popular use for the gadget, taking 12 minutes a day, only slightly longer than time spent writing and checking email (11 minutes) and text messaging (10 minutes).
- Several years ago the *New York Times* declared that nobody used the phone any more! (Paul, 2011)

How we use the telephone now and why this is changing

Do you have a telephone? No, I don't mean the phone that you carry around with you but rather a landline. The chances are that you don't. Most young people do not have a landline and do not intend to get one. For many millennials the home phone is a thing of the past and for older people a landline may be only useful for accessing broadband or relevant for businesses. Even most small business owners tend to use mobiles over landlines.

Telephone communication may be slower than its new media counterparts, but it still has benefits in an increasingly impersonal world. The telephone call, which connects a caller with a human voice, is still important.

Whether or not you use a landline, you do have a phone that can be used for voice calls but just how often do you do this?

Phone calls can feel awkward and intrusive. Whereas people once received and made calls with friends on a regular basis, we now coordinate most outings and social events via email or text. It's becoming common now in the workplace to make phone call appointments. More often than not, if you do make an unscheduled phone call you will only reach voicemail. On top of this the chances that the receiver will actually listen to your voicemail are also slim (Son, 2015).

Why is this? When most people see a voicemail from someone they do know, they either text the person back quickly or they'll immediately call the person back. They still don't listen to the message. What most people want is to feel that they're in control. When you take a phone call or listen to a voicemail, it can feel a little unpredictable. When someone calls you, you don't know if it's going to be a short confirmation, or if it's going to be a 30-minute conversation that significantly detracts from everything else you're working on. People want to be in control of themselves and their own schedule. We are using the phone less and less.

The not-checking-voicemail phenomenon makes for an interesting study in human behaviour. People instant message and text all day, hundreds of times, with strangers, friends, colleagues, clients, etc. But the majority of people do not want to take an unscheduled time out of their day to listen to the wants and needs of others. Voicemail doesn't integrate well with a person's average day, and because of that it gets neglected. This is part of the reason both Coca-Cola and JP Morgan have cut voicemail from their corporate offices (Son, 2015).

According to research conducted by accountancy firm Deloitte, the decline of voice conversations, which is particularly prevalent among those in their teens and twenties, may have an effect on interpersonal skills and job prospects. A Facebook update or chat is fast replacing a natter at the end of the day, and if you use a taxi-hailing app you do not need to speak to a taxi driver.

If it becomes easier and easier to message, what does that do to conversational skills where an immediate response is required?

Real-time communication

When we use the telephone we are communicating in real time which is different from how we communicate online, in the sense that we have far more information available to us through use of our voice and tone and how effectively we are listening.

Our brain has two ways of experiencing the world – one is by judging whatever we are experiencing through the filter of past experiences, perceptions and judgements, and this part of the brain is more activated when we are under stress or are feeling anxious. The other way we are capable of experiencing the world is a more direct way which allows us to get closer to the reality of any event. This happens by being present in the current moment. When we do this we are able to notice far more which means our interpretation of a message is more likely to be accurate. Revisiting the communications model from Chapter 1, if we are able to notice more real-time information we are cutting out some of the 'noise', so we are decoding messages more effectively and can be more flexible in how we respond.

We can notice more when we are in the present and this is helped through mindfulness, breathing and filtering out distractions – for more on this, review Chapter 2 on overcoming distraction.

Why is this important? Experiencing information in real time can make your telephone calls far more effective as you are less likely to be distracted by other activities or thoughts and/or judging incoming information through past experiences or future worries.

One added bonus of experiencing information in real time and being present is an immediate boost to your wellbeing and happiness levels too!

Good reasons to make or receive a phone call

Short of talking with someone face-to-face, a phone call is often the best way to get a personal response. If the person you called is available, you can take care of business on the spot. With other forms of communication, such as texting or email, you leave a message and hope for a quick response but you may not get one as quickly.

Assuming you can make a call and reach someone then phone calls may sometimes be the best method of getting your message across so it's a skill worth developing. Sometimes job interviews are conducted by telephone or Skype. Employers usually use telephone interviews when they receive a lot of applications or are recruiting for a lot of positions. It's a way of narrowing down the candidates into a manageable number that is possible for them to interview face-to-face. Equally you may be asked to take part in a Skype interview when you have been shortlisted for something. Overall, the chances of you being interviewed by phone are fairly high.

We spend a lot of time and energy preparing for face-to-face interviews so why do we seem to give less focus to telephone interviews? It's partly because we tend to avoid using the phone for calls generally and when we do use it our conversations tend to be very clipped and short – in fact they aren't really conversations as such but more like information exchanges. As mentioned above, more often than not these days you have to schedule a telephone conversation – that is, send an email first to make a date for a phone call – so it has somehow become invasive to just pick up the phone and ring. Other times, though, it can be really important to be able to pick up the phone, ring and then speak to someone – for example, if you are having trouble on a website, need to change a delivery time or make a special request, or are late for an appointment. We do still use telephones!

Speaking on the phone is becoming a less dominant form of communication and can cause anxiety mainly because you have to respond in the moment. There is no option of editing yourself, which is what you can do with virtually any other communication tool.

It has become very easy to hide behind email. Email is great for lots of things – see Chapter 4 for a detailed look at it. However, email is *not* good for conveying warmth and it is warmth that is essential for building trust. When miscommunication happens in texts and emails it's not random. It's usually as a result of reacting too fast. If you want to build relationships, aside from meeting face-to-face, the telephone is going to be one of the best mediums to use. And responding in the moment is good as it encourages us to be more present, more real and activates that part of our brain which supports this.

Here are some ideas for getting more comfortable with making telephone calls:

1) Commit to making the call in advance.

Try making an 'if-then' plan. This means creating rules for yourself for when you will use the phone. This means getting very specific about exactly what you are going to do and when you are going to do it. The 'if' is the situation – what are the specific circumstances when you really need to pick up the phone and call? The 'then' is what you're going to do – in this case pick up the phone. Here's an example: 'If I need to cancel an important appointment or meeting, then I'm going to pick up the phone.' That's it. You may wonder how that can be useful but actually you're four times more likely to follow through on your intention if you spell out exactly what you're going to do and when you're going to do it. That is because the if-then plan stops you having to rely on your willpower (remember that's a resource that steadily depletes throughout the day – discussed in more depth in Chapter 3 – *Working Smarter*) and willpower is a notoriously unreliable method of making yourself do things you don't really want to do. Willpower comes into play when you are not sure what to do and are trying to decide 'Should I call, or should I email?' – however, you won't have to ask that question because you've already decided that if you have to cancel something you are going to call. Imagine what a difference that makes when it is so easy (and often easier) to cancel by email or text and everyone does it! Taking the time to make a call instead can give a very positive impression.

2) Open with a question.

Often the beginning of the call, once you have got the greetings out of the way, can be the hardest part. Starting with a question is a great warmth indicator because it says that you are interested in the other person. Instead of barrelling into conversations with your agenda, start by putting the focus on the other person. If you know them, follow up on what they've been up to since the last time you spoke. 'I remember last time I saw you, you were working on X', or 'How are things going on that project?' If you don't know the person, kick things off with a question anyway.

The payoff is twofold. Firstly, you will be perceived as warmer and more trustworthy.

Secondly, asking questions can actually help you to feel less nervous. By directing your attention towards your conversation partner, you'll feel more comfortable during the call and they are likely to perceive you as a better listener. However, if you are using light-hearted banter to build rapport but not 'feeling it' then quickly shift to business. Some people just aren't 'chit-chatterers' and prefer to get on with things. It is up to you to be able to 'read' these sorts of signals, which can be harder to detect on the phone but are nevertheless readable through tone of voice, pauses or a lack of ease in the conversation generally.

3) Don't overthink it.

It's tempting to write out a telephone script, but it's far better to do a little thinking in advance about exactly what you want to say and how you want to say it. For everyday things, just call – too much planning can make you feel like it's going to be more difficult than it is. Remember that actually the best conversations happen when we are fully present, which means we're listening to what the other person is saying, and we're asking questions, and we're letting the conversation happen and unfold naturally. It's a two-sided affair. The best conversations aren't choreographed. Remember that if you are fully present you will naturally notice more and be able to respond more creatively and even in unexpected ways that could benefit the whole exchange.

If you feel you really do need to prepare then it's more effective to write your set of bullet points on paper before the call. Write out the reason you're calling, your key points and what you are requesting (if you are requesting something) in advance, as well your time allotment so you can always refer back and make sure you're keeping track and not forgetting key points.

4) Embrace authenticity.

What email and texting have done is raise the bar in terms of what we assume a good conversation looks like precisely because we are able to edit ourselves. But those expectations are simply unrealistic on the phone. Conversation is not a performance. It needs to be personal, real and genuine for it to be effective as a communication tool. So that means you need to be present and real too.

Make sure it is clear why you are calling. If you're calling for a specific reason then let the other person know what that is – it's as simple as saying, 'Listen, the reason I am calling is …'

If you're ringing for a chat, especially if unscheduled, then do check if it's a convenient time to talk, i.e. 'Are you OK to talk now?' or 'Is now a good time for you?'

5) Keep your eye on the big picture.

Your call may not go as expected and if that happens then simply take a step back and look at the bigger picture. You will develop your telephone skills only by making calls and learning what works and what doesn't. The more you do it the more confident you will become. Don't forget that everybody's on the same path. Even someone who comes across very confidently and smoothly will have had their share of calls that have gone wrong. What's important is adopting that growth mindset (see Chapter 3 – *Working Smarter*). If a call goes poorly or not as well as you had hoped for, spend some time thinking about what you can do differently next time and learn from the experience. The next call you make will be better.

The power of your voice

One of your most important tools for great telephone calls is your voice. We communicate lots of nonverbal cues through our voice: tone, volume, cadence and speech patterns. We can control our voice – its pitch and its tone – but this also requires building our own awareness of how we might be coming across.

Self-check

How would you rate your phone skills in a professional setting on a scale of 1 to 5 (5 = excellent, 1 = needs work)?

_____ **Warmth:** Do you sound friendly, warm and approachable on the phone?

_____ **Competence:** Do you sound competent and credible on the phone?

_____ **Confidence:** How confident do you sound on the phone?

_____ **Effectiveness:** How effective are your phone conversations?

Try this

Everyone has a natural range of voice tone. Are you aware of yours? Some people, when they answer the phone, tend to use a very high pitch. When you answer the phone or talk to someone in a higher pitch you could be signalling to them that you are not competent, mature or dependable. Why? Because we tend to associate high voices with children. So to talk confidently on the phone try these two immediate actions:

1. Stay in your lowest natural range of your voice. You can do this by taking a deep breath in and then slowly letting it out as you relax your shoulders, neck and head. Do it again and this time say 'Hello' on your out breath. It is impossible to speak in your higher range when your shoulders and vocal chords are relaxed – that's what you want. If you find yourself getting nervous on a call or your voice begins to crack, take a deep breath and speak on the out breath as you lower your shoulders. This will drop you down into a more mature tone.

2. Be aware of inflection. Don't use the question inflection. Another way we signal confidence is by telling someone our ideas as opposed to asking. When talking to the other person be sure your voice goes down at the end of your sentence instead of going up.

Back in Chapter 5 on face-to-face communication we discussed the importance of our voice tone. In speaking on the telephone, voice becomes even more important as it replaces some of the visual cues. In other words, we may use tone of voice more to help interpret the message if we cannot see the other person or their body language.

People cannot see us when we speak on the telephone, therefore judgements are made on what we sound like. The importance is not so much what we say, but how we say it.

- We assume others understand our meaning. Because you can't check facial signs of comprehension, make a special effort to ensure that the person you're talking to has grasped your message.
- Be aware of the tone you are using. People quickly make judgements about us based on how we sound and may pay more attention to this than the actual words we are using.

Diction

Diction is to do with how clearly you speak. It's not something we may be automatically aware of. Pronunciation is one area we tend to not necessarily focus on unless we are non-native speakers. In fact, it is something that we all need to be aware of, whatever language we speak! The words we speak are shaped by the mouth, particularly the lips. The vowels must 'carry' and the consonants clearly articulate. The lips and tongue have a specific job to do. When they fail to do this job, our speech becomes 'mushy' or 'mumbled' and words are unclear. Poor articulation can hurt your credibility when communicating.

Try this

An exercise in diction awareness

'Blind exercise' – pretending that you are speaking to someone who cannot see you, say the phrase, 'I'm glad to meet you.' Break each word down, concentrating on the following:
I'm (drop the jaw when attacking the 'I' for a more open sound) and be sure to close the lips on 'm'.
glad (finish the 'd' by putting your hand up to your mouth to feel for the quick spurt of air following the 'd').
to (the 'o' is given the sound of 'oo' and the lips should be pursed as if sucking through a straw).
meet (hum the 'm' and the mouth is in a smiling position for the 'ee'). Be sure to articulate the 't'.
you (the 'y' is a diphthong, meaning that two vowels are used to form this letter. Begin with a very quick 'ee', followed by 'oo') – ee-oo.

Practise this exercise until your speed and sound feels natural. It may feel odd at first but it will have an impact on your diction!

The role of oxytocin

Have you ever experienced talking to someone and feeling very connected to them? There is a physiological reason for this and it's connected to the hormone oxytocin. Oxytocin is more likely to be produced through eye contact and body language so it can be challenging to tap into this without seeing the other person.

In a business setting, one quick way to increase your levels of oxytocin when you are speaking to someone on the phone is simply by having their LinkedIn profile or website in front of you. This helps your brain feel that the person on the other line is a real person. This is also logistically quite useful because you can reference things about them as you speak. Doing this will also help your voice be warmer and will help you feel more connected. Whatever you do, if you want your phone call to be effective don't surf the web at the same time or 'quickly' check something. This may seem tempting and is quite common. It's important to keep your focus on the call and on the caller or recipient of your call if you want an effective outcome.

Another way that our voice tone sends positive or negative signals is through our emotions. When someone speaks to us with a lack of emotionality or tonal warmth we have trouble connecting to them. Remember from Mehrabian and Wiener's model in Chapter 5 that how you *feel* about someone or a situation is just as important as what you say and how you say it and each of these will have a bearing on your message. It's important to understand this as otherwise it will be tempting to project your feelings and emotions about a situation or person onto your communications, something we can do all too easily.

So make sure that when you speak with people you are sharing positive feeling and emotion through your words. How do you do this?

- **Tell stories.** When possible tell stories from your life, about your business and your past. Stories are wonderful ways of bringing emotion into your voice.
- **Elicit stories.** If possible encourage stories and ask questions. This makes a telephone conversation more engaging and feel more connected.
- **Share passion.** Talk about subjects, people and issues you feel passionate about. Don't temper down your feelings, express them. This is the basis of charisma. People who are rated as highly charismatic are extremely good at sharing their passions and getting excited about many subjects. They are also present and authentic.
- **Elicit passion.** Get the other person talking about topics they are passionate about. This makes the entire conversation more interesting, you more engaging and them more excited about the conversation.

Power posing

Have you ever heard of power posing? It can have a big impact on your confidence levels and therefore how you come across on the phone (or during a presentation).

Social psychologist Amy Cuddy is known around the world for her 2012 TED Talk, which is the second-most viewed talk in TED's history. A Harvard Business School professor and social psychologist, Cuddy studies how nonverbal behaviour and snap judgements influence people.

Body language affects how others see us, but it may also change how we see ourselves. Amy Cuddy's research into 'power posing' looks at how standing in a posture of confidence, even when we don't feel confident, can affect testosterone and cortisol levels in the brain, and might even have an impact on our chances for success. We send confidence signals with our posture. Power posing is an easy trick you can use to increase your testosterone levels. Power posing is when you expand your body to take up as much space as possible – even keeping your arms loose to gesture while you talk increases testosterone. Even just getting up and stretching or walking around as you talk will have the same effect.

The different ways we use telecommunication

A summary of telecommunication – each mode is effective in different ways:

Landline
- Still used in workplace offices and switchboards and can give a more professional impression if you are a small business or freelance.
- Better for certain clarity and clear connection.
- Conversations are likely to be more in-depth and planned in advance.
- Voice quality is better on a landline.
- However, also rapidly being used less and less at home.

Mobile
- Easy, affordable and accessible for phone calls.
- Can also be used for Skype and teleconference as well as for calls.
- Can be issues with connectivity.
- We are less likely to make phone calls using our mobile and when we do the conversations we have are short and transactional.
- We use our mobiles for a host of other ways of communicating, including texting and instant messaging which we will favour over a call.

Teleconference
- Still used often in business for meetings – more on teleconferencing in Chapters 7 and 9.
- Can be very efficient for linking people in multiple locations.
- Can be audio only, linked via telephones or by computer platforms.
- Varying degrees of interactivity depending on platform used.
- Can include video but typically the more people the less effective video will be.
- Many platforms exist which require training and familiarisation.

Skype
- Free and easy to use all over the world.
- Incorporates video and chat at the same time.
- Used for both personal and business use.

Most companies and workplaces will have preferences about what systems and platforms are used for online meetings and calls (more on this in Chapter 9 – *Online Meetings and Conferences*).

Basic phone rules

Be brief

However, do not be brief at the expense of making yourself clearly understood and not to the extent of sounding abrupt or discourteous. Lack of phone confidence often causes people to talk for longer than they would in a face-to-face conversation.

Be courteous

This is especially important because if you make a negative impression it will be very hard to correct later. Tone of voice is as crucial in conveying a courteous, cheerful impression as the words you use. And remember that your facial expression affects the tone of your voice so smile and try power posing! A smile can be heard – in the tone of your voice, which will sound pleasant and interested as a result. If you scowl or frown, your tone may come across as disinterested and unfriendly.

Be resourceful

Always think of ways in which you can be most helpful. If you are taking a message for someone else, use your local knowledge to suggest helpful ways of getting the caller and recipient of the message in touch with one another so that the caller can judge in an informed way what they want to do. At work, if the caller has been put through to your department and no one knows anything about the matter, think quickly. Who else in the organisation might know something and be able to help?

Self-check

How to build a positive phone personality:

- Don't worry about what you look like when you're on the phone and use as much body language as you wish to help build your confidence and your tone of voice.
- Focus your energy on what you are saying and what is being said to you.
- Mirror positive feelings in your facial expressions – if you smile while you're speaking there'll be a smile in your voice.
- Try to relax; stretch your muscles and breathe evenly because tension can feed straight into your voice and create a negative image.
- Avoid clichés like 'with all due respect' and 'between you and me' or 'to cut a long story short' that say one thing but clearly mean something else!
- Be aware that when you tell a lie your voice rises involuntarily and on the phone this is easily detected.
- Punctuate your conversation with 'you', 'your' and occasionally the other person's name.
- Replace some of your body language that you'd naturally use face-to-face (like head nods, quizzical expressions) with verbal equivalents like 'Yes', 'Of course', or 'I'm not sure I understood that last point. Could you…'

When it can be good to make a phone call

At the beginning of this chapter we discussed the fact that telephone calls are becoming less frequent. However, the telephone call is still used a lot and is certainly the best medium for certain types of communication. So, when is it better to use the telephone as opposed to messaging, texting, video conferencing or email? Well, short of face-to-face communication, making a call may well be the best medium to use – here are some reasons why:

Reason	Why
1. Telephones are more personal	
There may be times when it just makes sense to pick up the phone – this includes cancelling or postponing something, giving bad news, giving good news or checking how someone is. This also applies in the workplace.	While email and instant messages are often sent while the sender is multitasking, telephoning someone requires taking time out of your day to stop and make the call. This shows more care and demonstrates more attention.
2. Phone calls are often faster	
Even if you have to first schedule the call, the fastest way to deal with a question or key information can well be over the phone and means talking directly with the other person. You can save a lot of unnecessary texts and messages.	Messages can be conveyed more quickly over the phone than exchanging numerous messages by other means over the course of a day. When an immediate answer is required, a phone call is going to be the best way.
3. Meaning can get lost in translation	
Remember how we encode and decode information in the communication process (in Chapter 1 – *Your Amazing Brain*). If something is important it may well be best communicated by phone.	The main point here is that if the matter is important it is probably going to be best to use the phone. Also if a subject matter is sensitive and likely to be prone to misinterpretation via other methods then pick up the phone.

4. Everybody knows how to use a phone

Sure, you may need to practice your telephone manner but you know the technicalities of using a telephone and so does everyone else.

It's often difficult to keep up to date with all new communication methods and 'who is familiar with what'. Instead of having the difficult conversation about 'who's using what' or ensuring everyone is up to speed with a specific tool, you can make life simpler by picking up the phone.

5. Telephones are simple

There isn't any extra technology required apart from a landline or good mobile signal.

Using technology can often involve technical difficulties. Effective internet communication, using programmes such as Skype, require a reliable internet connection, non-faulty equipment and technological know-how. Things can and often do go wrong, whether we are in or outside of the office.

6. Phone calls can often be more authoritative

If you want to communicate an official message, deliver it with your voice.

Similar to how letters carry more authority, because of the traditional nature of a phone call it generally holds more weight than an email or an instant message.

7. Video calls can be awkward

Facial expressions can give things away and it can make working from home a little more difficult.

Sometimes being able to see the person to whom you're speaking is useful, but more often it's a hindrance and one extra thing to worry about.

Try this

1) Call five organisations – these can be companies you use for personal matters or companies from which you would like to have some key information such as where to address your CV. Make notes of how you are dealt with. What impression did this give you of each organisation?
2) Be a verbal detective – next time you make a phone call raise your immediate awareness by trying these:
   - Trust your intuition when picking up clues about the other person's personality, feelings and mood.
   - Stay relaxed and allow ideas about the speaker to drift into your mind; unforced impressions can prove to be remarkably accurate.
   - Look for hesitations, self-deprecating comments and other clues about the speaker's state of mind.
   - Check your understanding by replaying your impressions to the other person. Use 'reflecting back' phrases and practise active listening.
   - Use 'anticipatory feedback' to guide your conversation; imagine the other person's response to a statement you are about to make and then modify what you actually say to receive the intended result.

3) Decide on a particular piece of information you need; work out which firms or organisations might be able to help you and make phone calls (instead of checking their website) to get the information.

   If you are not successful in getting the information you need, analyse your phone method and try to work out why. Try again – for some new information. This exercise is very effective for perfecting your telephone technique even if the person you are calling keeps directing you back to the website! If they are good at their own telephone technique they should be doing everything they can to assist you and answer your questions.

4) Make a complaint about a recent purchase. Observe your own telephone technique (how successful you are in getting that voucher or discount or a refund) as well as the technique of the customer services person handling the call. Note any observations and what you have learned.

So what? How you can use the information in this chapter to boost your telephone skills

At the beginning of this chapter you may well have concluded that the telephone is hardly used anymore and that its use is diminishing even further. However, there is still wide use of the telephone and likely to continue to be. It is valuable to have good telephone skills because second to communicating face-to-face it can be your most powerful tool. Precisely because it is used less makes it important to use it well. As with online communication, speaking on the telephone does not provide us with nonverbal cues but the power of the voice is very strong. If we are listening carefully as well as using our voice effectively it can pack a powerful punch and go a long way to strengthening relationships as well as saving time, because we are exploiting the strengths of the multitude of different communication channels available to us.

Further reading

Blokdijk, Gerard. 2015. *Videoconferencing – Simple Steps to Win, Insights and Opportunities for Maxing Out Success*. Complete Publishing.

DeJoseph, Patricia. 2009. *Telephone & Cell Phone Communication Skills Handbook: (for Business & Everyday Life)*. Createspace.

Fisher, Jeremy. 2016. *This is a Voice: 99 Exercises to Train, Project and Harness the Power of Your Voice*. Profile Books.

Parrot, Terri. 2015. *Voice on the Phone: A Quick-Read Guide to Successfully Building Customer Relationships Using the Telephone*. Kindle.

Online Meetings and Conferences

What's in this chapter:

- Did you know? Facts and statistics about online meetings
- The rise of video conferencing
- The brain strain of audio conferencing
- Virtual teams
- How to run a great online team meeting
- The rise of one-on-one meetings taking place online
- So what? How you can use the information in this chapter to improve your online meetings

Did you know?

Facts and statistics about online meetings

- 32% of all meetings are conducted virtually (Absalom and Drury, 2014).

According to a 2009 *Economist* report:

- nearly half of all meetings are one-on-one. And more than one-third are virtual, with at least some participants attending from the road, remote offices or virtually anywhere with a phone or internet connection.
- 41% of virtual team members have never met their colleagues in a face-to-face setting.
- At least 25% of productivity depends on working virtually.
- The research also found that the top challenges during team meetings are: insufficient time to build relationships, speed and method of decision making, lack of participation and different leadership styles within the team.
- The era of the dominance of the PC and projector in the meeting room is coming to an end with employees increasingly taking devices such as tablets and laptops into meetings, blurring the lines between what is a physical and what is a virtual meeting.

You may be used to meeting people online in social settings and in a way we are meeting others online every day. In the workplace, though, online meetings are seen as an inexpensive way to get people together and if you have different offices in different countries or virtual teams which need regular contact then online meetings make sense. There are no travel costs and there is a host of user-friendly meeting software that make running and taking part in these meetings even fun.

There has also been a dramatic rise in the numbers of online meetings in the workplace. Today's employee is used to connecting online anywhere and often any time, too, via their mobile device or tablet using a host of online engagement and web conferencing tools. This makes it easy and straightforward to share screens and create and edit documents collaboratively as well as track team progress.

Self-check

1. Based on what you have read about communication so far, as well as what you know about technology, what are some of the things that might go wrong during an online meeting?

_____

_____

_____

_____

_____

_____

_____

2. Referring to Chapter 6 where we look in more detail at meetings, reflect on whether the essence of meetings is the same regardless of the platform (face-to-face or virtual).

_____

_____

_____

_____

_____

Your answers to the questions in the self-check box might include the following:

- Not being able to see others in the meeting means there is less chance for understanding body language and facial gestures.
- Lack of coordination – so everyone talks at once.
- Technology not working properly or lack of strong internet connection.
- People not being adequately prepared for the meeting – this happens both off- and online.
- The meeting not being taken 'as seriously' because it is online so there can be less attention/focus (i.e. multitasking).
- For any meeting, whether online or face-to-face, you still need a clear agenda and action points.

The rise of video conferencing

Video conferencing has been around for some time and with every wave of new technology and mobile working is only likely to increase. Generally, if you are taking part in a video conference or online meeting there will be a moderator on hand who is responsible for technical aspects of the call. However, this won't always be the case and it is important that you are familiar with the platform being used. You may or may not receive training on this and may be expected to familiarise yourself with the platform before the meeting by using tutorials or a guide provided.

Video conferencing may take place within a meeting room where you (and perhaps others from the company) will connect with others using the facilities and screen that are set up. Alongside this, and increasingly, you may well be taking part in online meetings through your own computer, tablet or mobile device using broadband and company software and these meetings may take place outside the work environment.

The advantage of video conferencing is being able to hold meetings with others who are in different locations. With video conferencing you can still see each other and so can, in theory, still pick up on facial expressions and body language.

However, your ability to 'sense' what others are conveying through body language does get lost. With video conferencing there is generally little time beforehand for informal chat and meetings tend to be more stilted than face-to-face because the tendency is to take turns to speak. This can impact our brain's need for 'relatedness' and to feel connected to those around us. Remember that this is the 'R' of the SCARF model outlined in Chapter 1.

The importance of rapport

We're social animals, and we naturally form social groups and build relationships. These groups build mutual trust and form a barrier against the unknown. This leads to the production of oxytocin, which increases the positive feeling of trust and stabilises these relationships. This helps a lot if you are working in a team. Creating rapport is key to generating relatedness and can be as simple as shaking hands, using a person's name or chatting about personal interests. Deeper rapport can be achieved through active listening and demonstrating empathy.

So although you can't shake hands online you can still achieve relatedness by ensuring that rapport is created online through using some of the ways you might do this face-to-face such as using names, informal talk before the meeting and demonstrating that you are listening through your tone of voice (check Chapter 8 – *Using the Telephone* for more tips on the power of the voice).

The brain strain of audio conferencing

Although video conferencing is on the rise we still take part in multi-person conversations via audio conferencing and a substantial percentage of all online meetings or online conferencing is still done via audio only. However quite often these audio conferences are frustrating and conducted poorly due to a range of factors from the inability to work out who is speaking (and the more people on the call the worse this is), the problem of two people speaking at the same time, the participant who delivers a key insight only to find their phone is on mute, to the participant working remotely with lots of background noise.

Even when audio conferences appear to go smoothly scientists have found they are rarely as successful as face-to-face meetings. Why? Because they force the brain to work in ways that are counter to its nature.

Our hearing evolved using incredibly sophisticated neural processing that allows us to hear the type and location of sound, which helps us interpret what we hear. Is the sound coming from a predator or from a baby, friend or foe, competitor or collaborator? Spatial and other subtle kinds of cues are missing from audio conference call technology, where the audio quality tends to be poor, every voice seems to come from the same location, and participants hear only the loudest individuals.

According to Dr Mike Hollier of Dolby Laboratories, an expert in auditory science and engineering, without this important data workers' brains have difficulty understanding what's being said, by whom. Hollier says:

> The part of the brain responsible for our conscious intelligence, the lateral prefrontal cortex, is very small relative to our entire intelligence. In fact, if we visualize our entire cognitive capability as the size of a football field, then our conscious intelligence – the portion of our intelligence that's available in the moment – would be the size of a tiny grain of sand. (Dolby Voice, 2014)

In face-to-face meetings, we don't need to strain our conscious intelligence to work out who is speaking or what they're saying. That processing happens automatically. But conference call audio is so hard to decipher that we need to devote our conscious intelligence to analysing audio information. With our conscious intelligence so taxed, paying attention to the subject of the conference call itself becomes exhausting.

It is clear from this that if we are taking part in audio or video conferencing we need to up the ante on our brain in terms of listening and focus and be aware that we will need to work harder.

See the table for tips on some simple things to do.

Tips for the chair or facilitator	Tips for all participants
As with any meeting do send an agenda or list of topics to be covered in advance as well as the names of who is in on the meeting. With some platforms, names of participants will be automatically added when they accept the invitation to the call. Send ahead any documents or visuals that might need to be consulted and make sure you have participants' contact details and emails to hand so you can send additional materials during the meeting if needed. As soon as everyone is online, hold a virtual roll-call and announce any extra arrivals or departures as they occur. Always address participants by name to make sure your comments and remarks are picked up by the right people. Sum up regularly to ensure that everyone remains in step and on track. Try to keep track of who's been silent and draw them into the conversation. If you can, avoid having too many people on the call in the first place (although of course this may not be something you are in control of). As with any other meeting, follow up with a thank you and any action points to be taken further. If appropriate also provide a brief summary of the meeting.	Make sure you have prepared for the call and are up to speed with any documentation or agenda. It's a good idea to have a hard copy of documentation or have it open on your screen. Do not 'switch off' and start doing something else during the call, however tempted you may feel! Make sure your email and messaging services are off too. Be aware of who is on the call and try to remember names. When you ask a question make it clear to whom you are talking. Remember you will need to listen keenly. If you are speaking why not quickly say your name when you contribute for the first time. Don't talk at the same time as someone else; pause for a second or two before speaking to make sure the other person really has finished. If someone asks a question, always reply, even if you don't have an immediate answer. Respond so as to ensure that it is clear you are listening and have heard the question. Make sure you are clear on any actions you have agreed to or that have been assigned to you.

Try this ✎

You work as part of a team that organises children's theme parties and have been asked to take part in an audio conference call to discuss the design of some new online marketing materials. A brainstorming face-to-face meeting has already taken place and you have been sent a summary of the ideas that were discussed. This audio call is to 'meet' the marketing copywriters that have been engaged to produce content and to decide on how to best proceed.

How will you prepare for the audio conference?

_____

_____

_____

_____

_____

_____

Virtual teams

Virtual teams can be defined as a group of individuals who work across time, space and organisational boundaries, and interact primarily through electronic communications. You may well have done some virtual team working during your studies or at least may be familiar with working and meeting online with other team members for a group project.

As we continue to work in a globalised world fuelled by technology we are also able to, and increasingly do, work across different time zones and countries. There are a number of reasons for the rise of virtual teams, but it has primarily been advanced digital technology that has made this a reality. Globalisation has made virtual teams a necessity. Once companies launched virtual teams into their day-to-day operations, an unanticipated benefit was discovered: virtual teams were typically more productive. Communication is usually more difficult, though, especially with global virtual teams, which can also aggravate the challenge in overcoming cultural barriers (Ale Ebrahim et al., 2009).

A recent report on virtual teams by RW[3] LLC, a cultural training service, found that 46% of employees who work on virtual teams said they had never met their virtual team cohorts and 30% said they only met them once a year. The report was based on a survey of nearly 30,000 employees from multinational companies. The survey also found that:

- the top challenge for virtual team members was the inability to read nonverbal cues;
- most virtual team members said they don't have enough time during virtual meetings to build relationships;
- there can be an absence of collegiality among virtual team members;
- it can be difficult to establish rapport and trust in virtual teams;
- managing conflict is more challenging on virtual teams than on conventional teams;
- decision making can be more challenging within virtual teams than conventional teams;
- it is more challenging to express opinions on virtual teams than on conventional teams (Hastings, 2010).

Generation Y (age ranges 26 to 35) are conducting a relatively greater portion of their meetings in a virtual capacity, averaging 38%. Predictably, these young professionals are relatively more comfortable communicating and collaborating in a virtual space and you may well identify with this and do this already. What is certain, though, is that you will definitely be working like this when you enter the workplace.

Self-check

Have you ever taken part in a virtual team meeting?
What were some of the difficulties you experienced and how were these overcome?
If the meetings went well what were some of the reasons for this?

How to run and take part in an online team meeting

Many of the same tips apply as for how to have successful meetings and you can read more on this in Chapter 6. Online meetings, however, because they lack the face-to-face element and because of technological considerations, do require a different approach and there is more to manage. It will become more and more commonplace to run meetings online and the rise of virtual teams also means you may well be working and doing business with people whom you may have never met face-to-face!

Before the meeting

Make sure the video is turned on. Usually everyone on the call is separated by distance, so the best way to at least feel like they're in the same room is to use video. There are many different platforms to choose from and your company may well have their own system or you will be using a collaborative Cloud tool.

Video makes people feel more engaged because it allows team members to see each other's emotions and reactions, which immediately humanises the room rather than it being just voices on a telephone line. Facial expressions matter, as we know, and you can read about this in more detail in Chapter 5 – *Face-to-Face Communication.*

However, if the meeting is being conducted without video then you will need to make even more use of your listening and communication skills and it will be even more important for the meeting to be facilitated effectively – have a look at the meetings section in Chapter 6 for more ideas as the same applies, and perhaps more so, for meetings online.

Have less reporting. Too many meetings, virtual and otherwise, consist of participants reading to each other around the table – and that can be a waste of the valuable time and opportunity of having people in a room together. The solution is to send out a simple half-page in advance to report on key agenda items – and then only spend time on it in the meeting if people need to ask questions or want to comment. This is also a good practice for large face-to-face meetings.

This kind of pre-work also gets people into the right mindset for a meeting as it encourages them (and their brains!) to start thinking ahead about meeting content and helps produce more ideas. What is important, though, is that everyone taking part in the meeting actually does read whatever has been sent in advance! Now, if you are not in charge of the meeting you may not be able to ensure this pre-work happens but why not suggest it to your line manager?

Come prepared with opinions. We already know that meeting preparation is important and makes the meeting far more productive. Always make sure you are familiar with the agenda and have discussed or had some input into what is going to be covered. What happens all too often is that people take part in virtual calls with a point of view, but because they haven't done any real homework before the call, they end up reversing their opinions once the call has ended and they've learned new information that they could have easily obtained in advance. Simply put, the more you have prepared the less opportunity there is for miscommunication and misunderstanding. Remember the communication model in Chapter 1 and how we decode messages – the moment we are online a whole host of other elements come into play that make it harder for us to read the environmental cues that we have when we are face-to-face. So focused and conscientious preparation is vital as well as working hard during the call itself to be present and focused.

During the meeting

People need to connect. People perform better when they are comfortable with each other, which makes for a greater degree of honesty and mutual interest. If you are leading the meeting (and you may not be), then part of your role, particularly when people may not know each other, is to help them to feel connected so you can have a productive meeting. How do you do this? You could do a personal-professional check-in at the beginning of each meeting. Have team members take one minute and go around to talk about what's going on in their lives personally and professionally. Go first to model the approach for what doing it 'right' looks like, in terms of tone and honesty. Remind everyone to respect each other by not interrupting and to only say what they're comfortable sharing with the group. And if you are not the leader you can always put this forward as an idea. Remember also that if you are able to suggest ways to make an online meeting more productive you are showing initiative and value and this may well be welcomed. Virtual meetings are still sufficiently new that there are no real 'rules' as such yet.

At the same time be aware that your company may have a specific way of running virtual meetings so listen out for opportunities to make your suggestions!

Encourage collaborative problem solving. A collaborative problem-solving session could be a much better use of meeting time. It's when the leader raises a topic for group discussion and the team works together – and sees each other as sources of advice – to unearth information and viewpoints, and to generate fresh ideas in response to business challenges. Again, this may or may not be something your company does and you may not have control of this but equally you may be leading a team meeting or can help to influence its direction.

Give each person time on the agenda. Along with collaborative problem solving, giving each person time on the agenda fosters greater collaboration and helps get input from all the team members. Here's how it works: in advance of the session, have team members write up an issue they've been struggling with and bring it to the table, one at a time. Each team member then gets five minutes on the agenda to discuss his or her issue. The group then goes around the meeting so everyone gets a chance to either ask a question about it or pass. After the team member answers everyone's questions, people then get an opportunity to offer advice in the 'I might suggest' format, or pass. Then, you move on to the next issue. It's a very effective use of a collaboration technique that could easily be managed in a virtual environment.

Careful with the mute button! In any meeting, there are social norms; for example, you wouldn't get up and walk around the room, not paying attention, at a face-to-face meeting. Virtual meetings are no different: you don't go on mute and leave the room to get something although this can and does often happen! In a physical meeting, hopefully you would not make a phone call and 'check out' from the meeting. So in a virtual meeting, you shouldn't press mute and respond to your emails – this will kill any potential for lively discussion, shared laughter and creativity. You will miss a lot of opportunities to engage and interact if you do this, not to mention information that may be vital. The rule should be that if you wouldn't do it in person then don't do it virtually, even if you see others doing it. And if you are leading the meeting make sure that this kind of behaviour is not acceptable. If at all possible it's good to agree these rules upfront.

Discourage multitasking. As we know from Chapters 2 and 3 on overcoming distractions and working smarter, multitasking was once thought of as a way to get many things done at once. However, it's now being increasingly understood as merely a way of doing several things poorly as you are switching attention from one thing to another rather than retaining focus. As science shows us, despite the brain's remarkable complexity and power, there's a bottleneck in information processing when it tries to perform two distinct tasks at once. Not only is this bad for the brain; it's bad for the team. Being mentally present is crucial for virtual team meetings to work. Again, you may not been in charge of this but you are in charge of your own behaviour. Here are some ways multitasking while at an online meeting can be avoided:

- Use video. It can essentially eliminate multitasking, because your colleagues can see you.

- Have the meeting leader call on people to share their thoughts. Since no one likes to be caught off-guard, they'll be more apt to pay attention.
- Give people different tasks in the meeting, rotated regularly. To keep people engaged, have different team members keep the minutes of the meeting; track action items, owners and deadlines; and even come up with a fun question to ask everyone at the conclusion of the meeting.

It's worth reiterating that when it comes to online meetings there aren't any hard and fast rules – it is up to companies to establish the best ways of running these, and in today's workplace that may well be you taking the initiative and making suggestions or, if leading a meeting, to find ways of making them engaging, on track and productive just like a face-to-face meeting.

The rise of one-on-one meetings taking place online

The most common online meeting taking place is the internal one-on-one meeting. With many employees working remotely or across time zones these are seen as important for building a positive workplace culture and often take the place of the traditional 'water cooler' conversation. In traditional offices, workers might chat during breaks at the water cooler or break area but with the evolving flexible workplace there is a tendency for this to be replaced by online meetings instead. In some companies such meetings may even take place on a daily basis! The value of such 'water cooler' meetings is that employees will have an opportunity to let off steam, chat through ideas and air opinions openly, often leading to breakthroughs and stronger team cohesion as a result.

As businesses and employees become more internally and externally connected, this creates a looser atmosphere and structure. This is reflected in the rise of the ad hoc meeting, where rather than scheduling in advance to set a time and physical or virtual location, workers are arranging to meet more spontaneously instead. At the time of writing, across all meeting types, 35% of meetings are ad hoc and this number is rising (Absalom and Drury, 2014).

This high proportion of smaller, ad hoc meetings highlights an additional challenge traditional web conferencing tools pose to the modern worker: they're designed for use by large groups, not for highly connected employees more inclined to one-on-one collaboration. Do individuals really want to go through the convoluted process of setting up a web conference when they are just engaging with one person? No doubt this will have evolved within a few years and there will be new tools in place for these newer kinds of ad hoc meetings.

So what? How you can use the information in this chapter to improve your online meetings

Although you may be used to meeting people online, meeting online in the workplace is likely to be a different experience, where professionalism is expected. Each organisation is likely to have its own rules and systems for using these tools so make sure you are familiar with them and that they are part of your on-boarding. If you are working for yourself then you are still likely to be using video or audio conferencing – try and become familiar with using these tools. You may have used Skype for personal use but it's also increasingly used for business communication and sometimes even for interviews. We did not discuss webinars in this chapter but again these are another method for meeting online. It's worth attending webinars within your industry, if you don't already, simply to update yourself with trends and new developments as well as to become familiar with using different types of webinar software. Better yet, why not offer to present a webinar – perhaps you might find there is a need to create and present a webinar on the very topic of video and audio conferencing which means you could also do some research into various software and collaboration tools. The point here is to get familiar with the technology and with the platforms and to use them. Even if you are not yet working you can use video and audio conferencing to work with a project team and this will give you vital practice. It's worth remembering that once you are in the workplace it may well be expected that you are already familiar with these tools and that training to use these platforms may well be minimal. There's no better way to learn than hands-on.

Further reading

Lepsinger, Richard. 2010. *Virtual Team Success: A Practical Guide for Working and Leading from a Distance.* John Wiley & Sons.

Ross, Alex. 2016. *The Industries of the Future.* Simon & Schuster.

Susskind, Richard. 2015. *The Future of the Professions: How Technology Will Transform the Work of Human Experts.* Kindle.

Van der Hagen, Paul. 2014. *The 7 Habits of Highly Effective Virtual Teams: Make a Success of Your Virtual Global Workforce.* Van der Hagen Publishing.

The Power of the Pen

What's in this chapter:

- Did you know? Facts and statistics about writing
- Why do we write less now?
- Good reasons to write by hand
- Why you need to mind map
- Right-handed or left-handed?
- Handwriting – it's personal
- Three writing projects: gratitude journal, reflective journal, goal setting and life planning
- Setting SMART goals
- The skill of writing: the CV, the proposal and the report
- So what? How you can use the information in this chapter to boost your pen power

Did you know?

Facts and statistics about writing

- Writing by hand can boost your productivity and help with setting goals, and taps into a part of your brain that can help you make great decisions!
- Students who use longhand when they take notes remember more and have a more in-depth grasp of the material (Mueller and Oppenheimer, 2014).
- Are you right-handed or left-handed? Did you know that your right hand is connected to your left brain – responsible for language, judgement and intellect, and your left hand is connected to your right brain – responsible for creativity, empathy and perception? You can strengthen your brain by swapping which hand you use to write.
- According to a recent study, 44% of managers feel writing proficiency is the hard skill most lacking among recent college graduates (2016 workforce skills preparedness report by PayScale).

This chapter is a mix of information about the importance of writing by hand and writing tips for different situations. Although you may not write much by hand anymore, there are specific situations when it can be very good to do so. Good writing, whether by hand or not, is needed for all kinds of business communication – from report writing to setting goals, from simple emails to critical writing for essays and analysis.

Why do we write less now?

Before the advent of the typewriter, anything important – including history, registers, account books and correspondence – was written by hand. Probably when you were at school much was made of the need for 'good handwriting'.

But why? When was the last time you wrote a letter? When was the last time you picked up a pen to write anything? Apart from examinations, hardly anything is written by hand anymore. In the past few days you may well have scribbled out a shopping list on the back of an envelope or stuck a sticky note on your desk or made a few notes during a meeting but that is likely to be it. We have become so used to typing on a keyboard for all our communications, note-taking is now conducted across multiple devices with apps to help you sync between them and letter writing has become a lost art. So why write now – is there really any need to write anything by hand in today's workplace or even in everyday life?

Handwriting still forms an integral part of most education systems, mainly because most examinations are still handwritten. Despite the incorporation of technology such as iPads in the classroom, students still write notes and examinations by hand and students who are unable to write legibly and articulately are at a considerable disadvantage.

Regardless of the time-saving apps we have all become used to, a percentage of medical prescriptions are still handwritten, personal cheque books are still in existence at the time of writing (albeit not for much longer), and we still write inside greetings cards which are usually received with great pleasure.
The importance of good, legible, quick handwriting cannot be underestimated in exam performance, or for note-taking at meetings. Even where personal computing and the human art of writing overlap (handwriting recognition technology) the ability to write well is still important in this hybrid world of communication.

It may seem that typing on a keyboard is so much faster than writing by hand but writing by hand unlocks something in the brain because it is personal and unique to us. Writing on a keyboard has more speed and detachment and allows us to edit and rewrite instantly and as much as we want to. The actual process of writing forces your brain to process information in a different way so that you can work your way through an idea or thought and actually write something down. When you physically write something, a sentence, a reminder, a couple of sentences, it doesn't matter. It engages a different part of your brain which will help you to remember it for longer.

Self-check

When was the last time you wrote something down by hand?
What immediate opportunities are there for you write something down?

Good reasons to write by hand

1) **Writing notes by hand taps into cognitive abilities** that enable you to process the information in a different way than if you had written them digitally. Writing by hand helps rid you of the distractions of the digital world and allows you to express ideas and thoughts much more freely and creatively. Many writers swear by handwritten documents. When typing there can be a tendency to edit as you go along rather than letting your ideas flow. This can be counterproductive for the creative process. With a blank piece of paper, you tend to just write, get your ideas onto paper and leave the editing process until later.

2) **Pen and paper can allow you to think more freely** when doing things such as brainstorming. You have a blank page, a pen, and no restrictions as to where you can write, allowing you to link things together, circle important points and add side notes wherever makes sense. Many will argue that this can now be done electronically with ease, but as mentioned before the distractions introduced with a computer or tablet can often interrupt your creative flow.

3) **Writing things down can clear your mind for higher-level thinking.** Have you ever heard of 'morning pages'? Julia Cameron, an American teacher, author, artist, poet, playwright, novelist, filmmaker, composer and journalist, claims the secret to a productive day is actually a simple practice. Every morning, take a pen and three blank pages and write down whatever you want to fill those pages. Through doing this you are clearing your head (and your brain!) in preparation for the day's most important thinking. Another technique to try is simply writing down every task, activity and project you need to address. There's something about getting these kinds of things out of the brain and onto paper that frees you up for other activities, enables you to find solutions and helps you to get more done.

4) **Writing helps process emotions.** Writing down what's on your mind is a great way to work through inner conflict or process your feelings around a particular situation. It's similar to talking a situation through with a friend, except it's a useful way of strengthening your self-soothing abilities and enhancing your self-knowledge and awareness.

5) **It keeps a record.** Anyone who has ever written a diary or journal knows that reading back through these provides quite valuable insight into your thought processes and emotions. When you can look back and see how you've navigated your way through a situation this can give you strength and confidence to deal with other issues.

6) **Writing helps you think big.** Writing things down gives you space to think big and aim high. No matter what's going on in our outside world, when we write things down, we enter a world of possibility. Doing this helps us stay motivated,

and it reduces the chance that we fall prey to self-limiting beliefs. (Even if we do, we can keep writing things down to process our feelings!) When we write things down, we have a chance to explore dreams and ambitions that we might not feel safe revealing to anyone else yet. We also have a space to keep track of all our ideas and desires so we can return to them later.

7) **Write it down, make it happen.** As well as offering a space for exploring possibilities, writing our goals and ambitions down makes it more likely that we'll achieve them. As with any goals, they are most effective if they are SMART: specific, measurable, achievable, realistic and timed. These are all variables we can work out and commit to through writing. Writing down our goals is the first step towards making them a reality. It can also help us stay accountable. When you've outlined your SMART goal in writing, display it somewhere you can see for an extra shot of motivation.

Try this

Try planning your next day in advance on paper and writing by hand. You will create order out of chaos quicker with a list than with any other tool!

Create a useful list: before you go to bed this evening, write out the six most important things that you can take action on the next day. Unpleasant things should always go to the top of the list and be done first!

Why you need to mind map

Mind mapping is a great technique you can use for ordering ideas for a bigger project, report or essay. It's also great for managing your time and for quickly assessing any situation you may find yourself in and, yes, it's best done by hand!
Here's how to do it.

Step 1: Start in the centre of a blank page turned sideways (landscape format). Starting in the centre gives your brain freedom to spread out in all directions and to express itself more freely and naturally.

Step 2: Use an image or quick sketch for your central idea. An image is very powerful (as you may already know if you use social media) and helps you use your imagination. A central image is more interesting, keeps you focused and helps you concentrate.

Step 3: Use colours. They are as exciting to your brain as are images. Colour adds extra vibrancy and life to your mind map, adds tremendous energy to your creative thinking, and is fun!

Step 4: Connect branches to the central image and connect your second- and third-level branches to the first and second levels, etc. This is because your brain works by *association*. It likes to link two (or three, or four) things together. If you connect the branches, you will understand and remember a lot more easily.

Step 5: Make your branches *curved* rather than straight-lined. This is more engaging and motivating for your brain.

Step 6: Use one key word per line because using single key words gives your mind map more power and flexibility.

Step 7: Use images throughout. Think of each image you include as being worth a thousand words. So if you have only 10 images in your mind map, it's already the equal of 10,000 words of notes!

Is being right-handed or left-handed important?

Ninety per cent of us are right-handed and whether we are right- or left-handed is believed to be genetic. The brain is 'cross-wired' so that the left hemisphere controls the right-handed side of the body and vice-versa and hand dominance is connected with brain dominance on the opposite side.

Left-handed	Right-handed
RIGHT HEMISPHERE	LEFT HEMISPHERE
Music, art, creativity, perception, emotions, genius	Speech, language, writing, logic, mathematics, science
HOLISTIC THINKING MODE	LINEAR THINKING MODE

This brain dominance makes left-handers more likely than right-handers to be creative and visual thinkers. This is supported by higher percentages of left-handers than normal in certain jobs and professions – music and the arts, media in general (MacManus, 2003).

Which hand do you prefer to write with? If you try writing with the opposite hand you normally write with it may feel awkward at first but has a lot of benefits too!

Because brain mapping shows that creativity is housed in the right hemisphere of our brains, experts say we can stimulate this right brain through working with our 'wrong' hand. This also works for left-handers, as studies indicate that one hemisphere is active when we use our dominant hand, but both hemispheres are activated when we use our non-dominant hand.

Other research shows that regardless of which hand we favour, writing and drawing with the non-dominant hand gives greater access to the right hemispheric functions like feeling, intuition, creativity, and inner wisdom and spirituality. Beyond the jumpstart in creativity, using the other hand helps your brain to better integrate its two hemispheres.

Handwriting – it's personal

According to research from the National Pen Company in the US, your handwriting can give away clues about 5,000 different personality traits based on the way you space your letters, how you sign your name, and even how you connect the letter 'o' and 's' to other letters in a word. Handwriting is deeply personal. Many recruiters make use of graphology to analyse handwriting and some even request cover letters written by hand. If handwriting is neat, well presented and without grammar or spelling errors, it can say a lot about you before any face-to-face meeting happens! Remember that handwriting is an expression of who you are whether or not you believe in the graphologists.

How to write a cover letter by hand

Handwriting can seem like a lost art in a time when almost everything is done on a computer, so take the time to get it right if you are asked to submit a handwritten cover letter.

1) You can write the cover letter on the same paper that you use for printing out your CV and it will be easier to scan if that's how you are going to send it. (Make sure you check the requested format first.) You could also opt for a higher-quality stock paper to make a really good impression. Use black or blue ink and a good pen.

2) Practise your penmanship. If your handwriting isn't neat, practise writing by copying another document. Remember what you learned at school, and practise a few times until your writing is clear and legible.

3) Keep your letter short and focused on why you are the best candidate for the job. Relate your experience to the employer's requirements. The first paragraph of your letter should explain why you are writing, the second explains why you are qualified for the job, and the third thanks the employer for considering you for the job. To be sure it's perfect, compose your letter on your computer, spell check and grammar check it, then print it and copy it by hand.

4) Write a rough draft of your letter so you can see how the spacing, paragraphs and format look on the page.

5) Proofread your letter. The employer is evaluating more than your penmanship. They are going to be reading your letter for content and style as well. Make sure your letter flows before you write the final version.

6) Write the final version of your cover letter using a good quality pen. Leave room for your signature.

Exercise: writing projects to try

Try one or more of these. The only rule is to write by hand!

1) Gratitude journal

Try keeping a gratitude journal for a few days. Keeping a gratitude journal has been shown to have a high impact on wellbeing. Arianna Huffington, author of *Thrive: The Third Metric to Redefining Success and Creating a Happier Life* (2015) says:

According to a study by researchers from the University of Minnesota and the University of Florida, having participants write down a list of positive events at the close of a day – and why the events made them happy – lowered their self-reported stress levels and gave them a greater sense of calm at night. Gratitude works its magic by serving as an antidote to negative emotions. It's like white blood cells for the soul, protecting us from cynicism, entitlement, anger, and resignation.

Start small – just spend some time before you go to sleep or when you get up to write down what you are grateful for. These can be as simple as the sunshine that day, your pet and good health or specific things you are grateful for.

2) Reflective journal
Keeping a reflective journal can be a very effective way to process emotions and thoughts. You will gain an immediate awareness of yourself, your emotions and your behaviour which in turn can help you regulate and manage emotions and situations more effectively. You may also gain new insights into problems and come up with great new ideas too. See also Chapter 1 on using this kind of reflection process to help handle challenging communication situations.

3) Goal setting and life planning
There is a great book called *Write it Down, Make it Happen* by Henriette Klause – simply writing down your goals in life is the first step towards achieving them. Putting it on paper alerts the part of your brain that focuses and pays attention. Writing goals in a daily planner, a journal or even on sticky notes helps focus our attention on them and makes them more real. Remember that doing this unlocks part of your brain that is most likely to galvanise you into taking action.

Where do you start, though, when it comes to goal setting and life planning? It may also seem strange to talk about planning your life when there are so many things that are unpredictable and uncertain. We are often pulled in many directions, which makes it hard to accomplish even one small goal. However, writing down such blueprints for your life and setting out goals for yourself is a powerful and positive exercise and will have an impact even when there are unexpected changes or obstacles along the way (which there will be!). In fact, it's better and healthier to think of possible obstacles you may face. Obstacles to achieving goals can include things that are actually coming from you like fear of failure, fear of success and lack of self-confidence. An obstacle can be less threatening if there are potential solutions. So think about some real solutions to help overcome roadblocks in the path to your success.

To prioritise your goals, look at all areas of your life such as family, health, career, finances and leisure activities. Then decide what goal or goals in each area truly motivate you and will most positively impact your life.

Try writing down 10 goals and then identify one goal on the list that will have the greatest positive impact on your life. Transfer that goal to a clean sheet of paper and make a list of potential obstacles with solutions as well as additional information, skills and people you need around you to achieve that goal. Then put this information into a plan and start taking action. This approach is very practical and helps you get started towards achieving your goals.

Make SMART goals for best results

The SMART goals technique is the most popular method used for goal setting in the world today. This method is useful both personally and in the workplace.

There are a number of variations of this technique but the most common version states that a well-set goal should meet the following criteria: be specific, measurable, achievable, realistic and have a time frame. And, yes, if you can write it by hand you are more likely to put it into practice!

Specific

Your goal needs to be as specific as possible so add detail here – think of using 'what', 'when' and 'where' to help you write this.

> **General goal:** Save enough money to buy a car.
>
> **Specific goal:** Save X every month for X months until I can buy a car by X date.
>
> **Tip 1:** Think about your goal from start to finish, and plan out how to do it. Try to sum it up in one to three sentences while plotting everything out. Simple to remember, simple to follow.
>
> **Tip 2:** SMART goals work best if you're willing to stay committed. Get yourself a day planner to help you stay on track. Write your goal on the inside page as well as the steps involved. Track your progress as you go along.

Measurable

A goal should be easy to measure, so you can chart your progress along the way. If you're saving money, obviously you can check how much money you've saved by looking at your bank account. If you're trying to lose weight, you can watch the numbers on the scale go down. You should also set an 'end'; that way, you know when your goal is fully accomplished. An end can be a target number (like weight), or a target amount of money; anything that you can count down (or up) to.

> **Tip 3:** When measuring, set up checkpoints along the way. If it's weight, then your overall goal might be to lose 30lbs, but try setting up check points every 5–10lbs and give yourself a small reward for your hard work.
>
> **Tip 4:** Measure carefully. It's easier to keep a goal if you witness all the progress you have made, rather than just occasionally checking in when you remember.

Achievable

It must be possible for you to achieve your goal. Pick goals that you are willing to work for, and that you're going to stick with. Don't force yourself to become better at an interest or skill if you're not going in with a passion.

Working towards your goals requires inner motivation, not outer motivation. Remember that you should be doing this for you, your career, your company or your family – ultimately to better your life and surroundings.

> **Tip 5**: Write out a mission statement to yourself and put it where you can see it. Reminding yourself of why you're doing it is a great way to stay motivated.

Tip 6: When setting a goal, ask yourself why you're doing it. If the answer does not come back as 'for me,' you might want to reconsider.

Realistic

When you create a goal, make sure that it is realistic. Goals should be challenging, not impossible! Don't expect to be able to save enough money in a year to buy a car if you're starting from zero. However, setting goals that are not challenging will often not accomplish much of anything. Try to find the balance between challenging and impossible that works for you.

Tip 7: Don't be afraid to ask for help. Friends and family are often more willing than you expect to help you stay on track. Some people also use social media for reporting on progress – this can be quite helpful as it links to being accountable in some way.

Tip 8: Be flexible – it's OK to extend the time frame a little if you need to.

Timebound

Set an end date that you would like to achieve your goal by. Never use the phrases 'One day I want to …' or 'I want to eventually …' as these are too vague. Instead, pick a time frame. For small goals, days, weeks and months work fine. For larger goals, months and years are perfectly fine. This will help give you the little push that you need to achieve them.

Tip 9: If you achieve your goal early, you might want to continue on until your finished date. Especially if this involves saving money. Just think how much nicer it will be to have a little more saved up when the last day comes.

Tip 10: When setting a time to achieve your goal by, don't set the date too early – try to be as realistic as possible with your end date.

Try this

Focus on your goals every day. It's worth investing in a planner or diary you can actually write by hand in. This way you can plan smaller tasks that help you reach your goal and become part of your day. A daily focus means you are more likely to create success in bite-sized chunks and get closer to your goal.

If you're a visual person why not try creating a vision board with pictures, symbols and words relating to goals? Again, this can help tap into the creative, perceptive part of your brain and help propel you towards achieving your goals.

Think about creating a mission statement for your life – this may make it easier for you to set goals. A personal mission statement simply provides clarity and gives you a sense of direction in your life. See it as a map that will guide you to the life you want to have. When you're guided in life by this changeless sense of who you are, why you're alive and what you value in life, there are no difficult choices and you'll always know what the most effective use is of your time, your talents and energy.

The skill of writing

Regardless of whether you write by hand or digitally, being able to write well in the workplace is necessary. Any time a profession requires written communication, writing skills become important. You will use them in many situations at work.

Think about these:

Communication

With emails, notes, letters, texts and tweets, most people spend a fair amount of time at work communicating via the written word. Whether you are messaging a colleague, writing to your manager or crafting a newsletter, your writing skills can boost or hinder you easily, even if you do not have a 'writing' profession. Basically, writing skills make a difference in how you come across and apply in most industries and jobs. That means being aware of your style of writing, your use of grammar and your spelling.

Credibility

People with good writing skills are generally seen as more credible. Think to yourself how you would interpret an email from a colleague that was filled with typos and grammatical errors or not written clearly. At best, s/he might be considered negligent in that s/he didn't proofread the message or use a spell checker; at worst, s/he comes across as less intelligent and less capable. Better writers tend to be perceived as more competent and more intelligent than their less literary counterparts. This may not seem fair at all but it is all about perceptions and how you come across! Remember, too, that in the absence of being face-to-face we use other measures to interpret and decode information.

Considerations

In the workplace, you need to make sure that you proofread everything you write, from an email to a company intranet message. However, just because good writing skills are a plus, you still need to pick your battles. Correcting others can work against you or be perceived negatively. Further, context and tone are just as important as grammar. While obvious mistakes are a no-no, such as using 'their' and 'they're' incorrectly, smaller errors, like confusing 'who' and 'whom' may be perceived as less important.

With these in mind we are now going to focus on three documents you are likely to be writing in the near future and in the workplace: the CV, the proposal and the report. Each of these is different from the others and will have a different writing style.

The CV

It is likely that you already have a CV and will have had guidance on how to write one. As with many forms of communication that we discuss in this book there isn't necessarily a hard and fast way to write a CV and indeed conventions change all the time. So it is worth thinking about the context within which you are sending your CV and bearing in mind that recruiters and potential employers receive a huge number of CVs on a regular basis and throw an equally huge number in the bin without even looking at them. So fundamentals apply such as neatness, clarity, brevity, tailoring it to the position you are applying for and ensuring it is written well. A surprising number of CVs contain spelling mistakes, too, which can create a very negative impression.

Your CV needs to be a document that someone is interested in reading. At the same time, often the CV is a formality and merely part of a bigger bundle that will comprise a number of elements including pre-existing relationships and connections, your online presence and LinkedIn profile and the events that have led to you applying for that particular job. It is seldom worth sending out your CV unsolicited to large swathes of employers hoping for the best, and far more effective to send a CV to 10 companies to which you have some kind of connection already. You will hear differing advice on CVs and must make up your own mind about the best course of action to take. Remember that your CV is a marketing document in which you are marketing something: yourself! You need to 'sell' your skills, abilities, qualifications and experience to employers.

The following format can be used. As your career evolves your CV will too and will most likely highlight your experience and relevant expertise before qualifications. When you are just starting out, though, it's important to state your qualifications upfront.

Personal details: This is your name and address and optionally your date of birth. You may also include a photograph, which is increasingly common, as well as your LinkedIn address and website, if you have one.

Qualifications: If you have not yet graduated this should be your degree subject, your university and date of expected graduation. Include A-levels and even GCSEs, and if it's a first job do include grades though these are not always necessary.

Work experience: Use action words such as *developed*, *planned* and *organised*. Make sure you are highlighting your transferable skills. Even work in a shop, bar or restaurant will involve working in a team, providing a quality service to customers and dealing tactfully with complaints. Don't mention the routine, non-people tasks (cleaning the tables) unless you are applying for a casual summer job in a restaurant or similar.

Try to relate the skills to the position you are applying for: A finance job will involve numeracy, analytical and problem-solving skills so focus on these, whereas for a marketing role you would place a bit more emphasis on persuading and negotiating skills.

Example:

All of my roles have involved working within a team-based culture. This involved planning, organisation, coordination and commitment, e.g. in retail this ensured daily sales targets were met, a fair distribution of tasks and effective communication among all staff members.

Interests and achievements: Keep this section short and to the point. As your career evolves, your employment and experience will take precedence and interests will typically lessen in length and importance. For now, though, they can be used to give some information about the type of person you are.

Interests: CV dos and don'ts

DO	DON'T
Use bullets to separate interests into different types, i.e. creative, sporting etc.	Write continuous paragraphs as these can be difficult to scan.
Show a range of interests to avoid coming across as too narrow. Any hobby a bit out of the ordinary can help you to stand out – things like mountaineering or skydiving can show a sense of stretching yourself and coping well in demanding situations.	Highlight too many solitary interests such as reading or cinema as this might come across as lacking in people skills. If you do put these then say something about the kinds of books you read or films that you watch and why.
Mention any interests relevant to the job. My niece was headhunted for a presenting role for a new BBC YouTube channel based on her own YouTube channel where she had created many funny presenting videos in her spare time, and this made her stand out as well as easy to find.	Have a long list of interests that may well really be your interests but which are not relevant to the job. It's better to leave them out.
Mention anything showing evidence of employability skills such as team working, organising, planning, persuading, negotiating, etc.	Write long sentences, have untidy margins or use fonts that are too large.
Mention any evidence of leadership such as captain or coach of a sports team, a project leader or chair of a student society or club. Then say something positive about it: 'As student leader of the university theatre production I had to manage a diverse group of people, and project manage the production, budget and logistics.'	Mention interests without linking them somehow to transferable skills which are relevant or have been stated in the job description. Some recruiters use software to scan electronic CVs for keywords and if none are found the CV is immediately discarded.

Skills: Mention any pertinent skills relevant to the job here if you can. These could be digital skills, design skills, language skills and holding a driving licence. And maybe you have additional unique skills of interest like coding or touch typing.

References: Many employers don't check references at the application stage so unless the vacancy specifically requests referees it's fine to omit this section completely if you are running short of space, or to say 'References are available on request.' Normally two referees are sufficient: one academic (perhaps your tutor or a project supervisor) and one from an employer (perhaps your last part-time or summer job).

Remember that your CV is only one part of a whole package!

The proposal

What is a proposal and why do you need to know how to write one? You may have had to write a dissertation proposal but in the workplace this is a different kind of document. Proposals are written when people need to ask permission to make a purchase, conduct a project or write a paper; the proposal is a formal way of putting forth an idea and asking for action to be taken on that idea. Your ideas or suggestions are more likely to be approved if you can communicate them in a clear, concise, engaging manner. Knowing how to write a persuasive, captivating proposal is essential for success in many fields. A proposal is also written if you are pitching for freelance work or consultancy and if you end up with a portfolio career they may be the main method of obtaining work.

When writing a proposal, consider who will read the proposal and what that person may or may not already know about what you are proposing.

Planning stages in writing a proposal

This is one of the most important steps in writing a good proposal. You need to define your audience, or know who they are, and, if applicable, you need to be fully familiar with the proposal guidelines and criteria – if you are invited to submit a proposal for something then usually there will be pre-set criteria and guidelines to be followed. Like your CV, if these are not followed or there are omissions your proposal may never get past the initial stage of vetting.

So, think about your audience and what they might already know or not know about your topic before you begin writing. This will help you focus your ideas and present them in the most effective way. It's a good idea to assume that your readers will be busy, reading (or even skimming) in a rush, and not predisposed to grant your ideas any special consideration. Efficiency and persuasiveness are key.

At the planning stage it is also a good idea to set out a structure for your proposal. This may well be set by the proposal guidelines already so you can use these for headings and subheadings.

Conduct any appropriate research. This might be research that backs up your proposal in some way or helps you to better define the market, background context or argument for what you are proposing.

Brainstorming your approach

Another very important step. If you are writing anything – whether that is a book, an essay, a dissertation, a report or a proposal – *writing the actual document is the very last piece of work that you do!*

Now that you've done your research and laid the groundwork, brainstorm the situation and your approach. Doing this now will make your proposal much easier to write!

Use these questions to help you:

- What is the issue/problem/need/context?
- Why is this important?
- Who/what is affected by this?

- What is not being achieved due to this problem/issue/need?
- How will the proposal recipient measure the success of the solution? (This may be set out in the proposal documents.)
- Of these success measures, which is most important to the proposal recipient?
- What, precisely, are you proposing?
- How will you do this?
- What proof can you offer that you are qualified and competent and the best person to do this work?
- What quantitative promise (value proposition) are you willing to make?
- How can you demonstrate that the value you propose to offer is credible?

Having some answers to these questions will help you to formulate your proposal more effectively. This is a brainstorming exercise, not a writing exercise, so at this stage you are not writing but rather making notes or bullet points, or perhaps creating a visual board and using sticky notes. Working in this way helps your brain to categorise and order information more efficiently and can also uncover new ideas, whereas if you start actually writing the report too quickly and too early it won't be as effective.

Write the executive summary

Contrary to popular belief, the executive summary is *not* a summary of the contents of the proposal. It is a summary of the basic issues, the proposed solution and the promised results. Effective executive summaries are structured like this:

Problem, need or goal

Expected outcome

Solution overview

Call to action

Now write the body of the proposal

The body contains detailed explanations of how you will do the work, the people involved, the prior successful experience you have in this area, previous customers you've helped on similar projects, and evidence of your core competency and financial stability.

In many cases, your target audience or client will have already defined the structure of the proposal or provided a template. If so, follow that structure exactly. Remember, too, that most decisions are usually made based on the executive summary, but failing to follow a template automatically disqualifies you, regardless.

The report

What is a report and why do you need to learn how to write one?

Reports are generally business documents that are written for a clear purpose and for a particular audience. Specific information and evidence are presented, analysed and applied to a particular problem or issue and the report is usually research based. The information is presented in a clearly structured format, making use of sections and headings so that the information is easy to locate and follow.

When you are asked to write a report, as with a proposal you will usually be given a report brief which provides you with instructions and guidelines. The report brief may outline the purpose, audience and problem or issue that your report must address, together with any specific requirements for format or structure. Like the proposal it will be very important that you follow and adhere to this structure.

A well-written report will need to:

- show understanding of the purpose of the report brief and adhere to its specifications;
- gather, evaluate and analyse relevant information;
- structure material in a logical and coherent order;
- be presented in a consistent manner according to the instructions of the report brief;
- make appropriate conclusions that are supported by the evidence and analysis of the report;
- make thoughtful and practical recommendations where required.

Most reports will follow a similar structure:

Heading/title or subtitle	Content
Title page	This should briefly but explicitly describe the purpose of the report. It should also include your name, the date and the person for whom the report has been written. There may be a department but generally there will be a specific contact to send the report to.
Terms of reference	This heading will include a brief explanation of who will read the report (audience), why it was written (purpose) and how it was written (methods). It may be in the form of a subtitle or a single paragraph. It may also include terms of reference that were set out in the original report brief.
Executive summary	Like the proposal this is an important part of your report and will likely be the only part which is read in full. The summary should briefly describe the content of the report. It should cover the aims of the report, what was found and what, if any, action is called for. Your conclusions and recommendations should be summarised here. The executive summary should be no longer than one page and avoid detail or discussion; just outline the main points. Remember that the summary is the first thing that is read. It should provide the reader with a clear, helpful overview of the content of the report.
Contents/Table of contents	The contents page should list the different report headings together with the page numbers. Your contents page should be presented in such a way that the reader can quickly scan the list of headings and locate a

	particular part of the report. You will need to number headings and subheadings in addition to providing page references. Whatever numbering system you use, be sure that it is clear and consistent throughout. Make sure you don't leave this task to the very end of your deadline – producing a table of contents takes time and if you get it wrong it can make a negative impression on the reader.
Introduction	The introduction sets the scene for the main body of the report. The aims and objectives of the report should be explained in detail. Any problems or limitations in the scope of the report should be identified, and a description of research methods, the parameters of the research and any necessary background history should be included.
Methodology	Information here will include the sources of your research, how evidence was collected and what methods you used.
Findings	This section should include a summary of the results of your work together with any necessary diagrams, graphs or tables of gathered data that support your results. Present your results in a logical order without comment. Discussion of your results should take place in the main body (discussion) of the report.
Discussion – this may well be split into specific subheadings of themes depending on the subject, nature and scope of the report	The main body of the report is where various themes or subheadings are discussed in much more detail. The facts and evidence you have gathered should be analysed and discussed with specific reference to the problem or issue. Your points should be grouped and arranged in an order that is logical and easy to follow. Use headings and subheadings to create a clear structure for your material. Use bullet points to present a series of points in an easy-to-follow list. As with the whole report, all sources used should be acknowledged and correctly referenced.
Conclusion	In the conclusion you should show the overall significance of what has been covered. You may want to remind the reader of the most important points that have been made in the report or highlight what you consider to be the most central issues or findings. However, no new material should be introduced in the conclusion.
Recommendations	If you have been requested to make specific recommendations these should be included here and clearly numbered together with suggested action points.
Bibliography	Your bibliography should list, in alphabetical order by author, all published sources referred to in your report. There are different styles of using references and bibliographies so you should check the preferred method of your company.
Appendices	This is where you would add any additional material relevant to the report.

This may seem, and indeed is, a long structure and it may also seem that any resulting report is likely to be very long. However, this depends on the nature of the report. Bear in mind that the executive summary is probably the most important component of any report and may be the only part that is read. Although it may seem rather unfair that your entire report is not read it is important to remember that, unlike your proposal, it will be impossible to write a good executive summary without having put in all the work for analysis and findings. So make sure you write your executive summary last. It's also worth bearing in mind that your report will certainly get read in detail by its specific audience whereas a wider audience may only be sent the first section of the report.

Some reports also require a presentation alongside them and increasingly many organisations are moving towards a far more interactive way of documenting and presenting reports. This may mean that the entire report, once written (and it will still need to be written first) may get 'translated' into an online platform of sorts where images, links to relevant material or appendices and key elements of the report are all accessed through clicking on a link or section rather than forming a traditional report.

Writing style for reports

Because of the way people digest information now, it is even more important to adopt a concise and direct style with reports. Avoid any unnecessary or descriptive language if you can. To get a better understanding of how to write reports, get familiar with the style your organisation uses. It should also be possible to access in-house reports on the company intranet.

So what? How you can use the information in this chapter to boost your pen power

This chapter has focused on writing, and in many ways it may feel like a lost art. However, it is a vital skill in business and the person who can write clearly, articulately and briefly will be prized. We have also looked at the power of writing by hand which may be something you had not considered before. Writing by hand can tap into a different part of your brain, enabling you to become more resourceful, creative and insightful in a way that tapping onto a keyboard cannot. Keeping a journal can be very useful and a great way of setting intentions and goals as well as a good way to note down ideas and use tools such as cognitive behavioural techniques (CBT) and reappraisal from earlier chapters. Most of all, writing is an expression of yourself and who you are and is part of what makes you unique.

Further reading

Greenhall, Margaret. 2010. *Report Writing Skills Training Course. How to Write a Report and Executive Summary, and Plan, Design and Present Your Report: An Easy Format for Writing.* Universe of Learning Ltd.

Klauser, Henriette, A. 2001. *Write it Down, Make it Happen: Knowing What You Want –
and Getting It!* Simon & Schuster.

Taylor, Neil. 2011. *Brilliant Business Writing: How to Inspire, Engage and Persuade Through
Words.* Pearson Business.

Putting it All Together

Much of the focus of this book has been on helping to raise your awareness of how we communicate and how this links with the thought processes in our brains. There is much that we can do to control how we come across to others, although of course we cannot really control how we are perceived. We can, though, influence how we come across to others by having a better understanding of the communication process and our brains in a range of settings.

Let's look at all this through the lens of a typical week in the life of a young woman we'll call Zoe. What we are doing here is 'compressing' the impact of Zoe applying her awareness of these skills and what might be happening in her brain to all of the communication scenarios she may experience within a working week. When you are in the workplace you will likely experience all of these communication scenarios – perhaps not all within a seven-day period, but certainly within a period of a few weeks.

We are also going to look at the week through two takes. The first take is Zoe going through her week with a lesser awareness about communication skills and processes and the impact of what may be happening in her brain because of these. Of course it is unlikely that the week would go exactly like this; what we are doing is applying a magnifying glass, imagining what a normal week in someone's life could look like compared with the second take where Zoe is activating some of the principles outlined in this book.

Zoe graduated from university a year ago and she is now in her first job working in a media communications company as a junior digital projects manager. You may be working in a completely different industry but the communication scenarios will, nonetheless, be similar.

In order to get the job in the first place Zoe will have undergone an interview process. Because interviews are likely to be very much on your mind at present and will be a frequent feature in your job searches, we'll first of all rewind a little to Zoe's interview for this job. Approaching job interviews needs to be quite a strategic process involving thought, research and a proactive stance.

If you are taking this approach you'll already know that probably the only time you should send a CV or résumé is when you've established there is a real job at a company for which you're being considered, or a headhunter is trying to fill an open position and requests one. Of course you may submit your CV to a number of different places without this but it's important to bear in mind that if you do this you are one of many, competition is fierce and it mustn't be your only approach.

It's also worth remembering that many recruiters prefer to simply look at your LinkedIn profile rather than at a CV. You can find out more about getting that

LinkedIn profile right in Chapter 7. And if you do have a CV it should be clean, clear, simple and no more than two pages. You can find out more about writing your CV in Chapter 10.

Back to Zoe:

Interview process: Take 1

Zoe has been fortunate in that she has received guidance and support at university on getting ready for the workplace. She knows she needs to have a well-thought-out and well-written CV and that she needs to be proactive when it comes to interviews. However, Zoe does find it difficult to be motivated. Beyond doing an internet search about media companies and the industry generally she has done little additional research.

She has a number of good leads and has been invited for interview at two great media companies. She feels strongly that she comes across well and is confident.

She does some research about the companies and has a fairly good idea of their turnover, business goals and business culture. When she gets the call for the first interview Zoe is very excited and animated and she straightaway accepts the interview date offered and the time they give her – she wants to appear keen and eager, right?

The night before the interview an old friend is in town. Zoe is very sociable – this is the one opportunity she has to see her friend so she arranges to go out for the evening to catch up – it's got to be good to relax before an interview and to celebrate the fact that she has got an interview in the first place. Zoe knows that if she has been invited for interview then she has already demonstrated that she has the right credentials for the job. The rest is just about establishing a good fit.

She feels relaxed the night before and has a few drinks with her friend. That night she sleeps fitfully and wakes up worrying about the interview. Why is she worrying? This could come from a number of areas which mean that her brain's limbic system (the part that feels under threat) is kicking into gear. Zoe may fear the unexpected: 'What if the interviewer asks me a question I don't know the answer to?' She may have 'butterflies' in her stomach just from the thought of being interviewed. A bit of nervousness and anticipation is good and may actually help Zoe perform better but it's not good when these kinds of worries come after a bad night's sleep. It's not a good way to start the day.

Nevertheless, Zoe gets up on time, showers and dresses and has a quick coffee. She has decided to wear a simple shift dress – it is high summer and she knows the media industry is fairly informal. Besides, it's Friday when most offices dress down anyway. Zoe is in a rush to reach the interview in time for her 9am slot.

The journey involves three train changes. Unfortunately, one of the trains is late which results in an overall delay to her journey. Zoe gets to the interview with minutes to spare and now feels very stressed. Her body's stress response kicks in more strongly now causing more anxiety, nervousness and tension. This makes Zoe's heart beat faster, her blood pressure higher and her breathing faster, too, because more oxygen and blood is being pumped into her system getting her ready for action – fight or flight, except Zoe is not in danger in this sense. What is happening is that threat signals are being sent to the brain resulting in the body creating hormones to help Zoe deal with the situation. The two primary hormones involved are cortisol (the stress hormone) and testosterone (the dominance hormone) (Chapter 1 – *Your Amazing Brain*).

The interview that Zoe's mind is now perceiving as a threat increases cortisol levels and lowers testosterone levels. This leaves her with an elevated heart rate, cold palms, sweaty armpits and a feeling of vulnerability and powerlessness. Definitely not what we need heading into a presentation, job interview or any high-stress social situation.

Zoe arrives at the company rather flustered, takes her seat in the waiting area and immediately hunches up her body and tenses her shoulders.

As Zoe enters the interview room she feels so tense that she isn't able to take in her surroundings fully or greet the interviewer as confidently as she might have. Even though she knows this is important, she is hardly conscious of it because of the way her brain has kicked into gear, flooding her body with hormones.

Zoe had thought of several key accomplishments to talk about that demonstrate her strengths of working within a team and meeting deadlines. She knows these are two important criteria for the job so it's important to have some examples up her sleeve. She is ready for that question about strengths!

She also knows she will likely be asked about her weaknesses. She has a couple of strong life stories to tell where she has overcome difficult situations. However, the stress in her body has now caused her to blank out these prepared answers.

Zoe gets nervous and tenses up. Her mouth becomes dry, she starts to sweat again and her brain starts to blank out even more. She manages to get through the interview and answer most of the questions but leaves without asking any questions herself.

On the way home all Zoe can think of is what she had intended to say, what she could have said and what did not go well. If we were to continue on through Zoe's day we would discover that her experience of the interview influences her entire day, causing more stress to the point where she is unable to relax and spirals into negative thoughts about how she 'bombed' the interview and is 'no good'.

Interview process: Take 2

The scenario is the same – Zoe has been invited for an interview at a great media company. She knows she comes across well, is qualified and likely a good fit for the job. This time she approaches the whole process in a different way because she knows that being confident and able to interact in the moment comes from her preparation and knowing how to handle her nerves, and that certain elements of this whole job search process are within her control. She knows she may get nervous but also knows that there are strategies she can use to help herself should that happen. Zoe also knows that by being prepared she will have more control over her nerves and naturally feel and come across more confidently.

So what does Zoe do in Take 2?

When Zoe gets the call for the interview she is overjoyed and excited. She knows that when she speaks on the phone her voice tends to get quite high-pitched and she remembers to slow down and to lower her pitch. Just doing this gives her a little more time to reflect – the day and time that the company is suggesting – 9am on Friday – is not ideal for Zoe because of the travel time involved. She very politely asks if a slot is available later in the day as she is coming from some distance. This allows her time to travel to the interview unflustered. It may seem tempting to accept the first available slot but Zoe feels it's worth asking for a different time if it means that she can plan for a smooth journey.

First of all, Zoe prepares thoroughly, making sure she really understands the company's core business operations, its strengths and its challenges. She does her own research on this and she also does a little research on sample interviews in the media industry, making sure she is familiar with the types of questions that might be asked rather than just generic strengths-and-weaknesses-type questions. Zoe thinks about her best responses to difficult questions and thinks about how she will deliver them – for example, she intends to take time to breathe deeply and pause to give herself reflection time before answering. Zoe then takes a further step and records herself on her iPhone practising these answers. When she listens back she hears that her voice tone gets a little squeaky in places so to improve her flow she writes down her answers and practices again, and on the third time she uses simple bullet points. Although this may sound like it would take up a lot of time, Zoe only spent about 30 minutes on it and included a few lines about her main strengths, matching them to the job description.

Rather than approaching this job interview with the goal of getting the job, Zoe decides to think of it as a vehicle for finding out if the company, the management and the job itself are a good fit for her skill set. Zoe also, based on her research, prepares a list of her own questions about the job role and about the company. Doing her homework serves two important functions in the job interview. Good questions provide Zoe with the information she needs to make a decision about the job, and hopefully they impress her interviewer. An effective manager will know that Zoe has done her homework by what kind of questions she asks. They realise that she understands what the job requires, because she's able to discuss its potential opportunities and challenges. When Zoe is asked if she has any questions at the end of the interview (and this is likely to happen in all interviews!), simply shrugging and saying 'not really' is not an option.

The day before the interview, Zoe gets a call from one of her best friends whom she has not seen for ages and who is in town only that evening and wants to meet up for drinks. Zoe knows that she needs to get a good night's sleep to function well the next day and be at her best. She explains to her friend that she has an important job interview the next day and agrees to meet for a quick coffee early evening. She returns home about 7.30pm, has a delicious healthy dinner and then gets to bed at a reasonable time. Zoe sleeps well knowing that she has prepared to the best of her ability. Yes, there will be unknowns tomorrow but Zoe feels able to handle these with ease.

So Zoe arrives on time at the interview refreshed, energised and relaxed. She greets the interviewer with a firm handshake and a bright smile. She is dressed appropriately in a pleasant work suit, neat make-up and polished shoes which she had laid out the night before. She had visited the company location a few days earlier so that she could road test the journey as well as make some observations about what company employees were wearing. Zoe knows that she has only a few seconds for this very important initial impression so she needs to manage them well.

During the interview Zoe does her best to engage in the conversation as an equal and is confident in answering questions. This gives an immediate favourable impression and Zoe comes across as knowing how to express her thoughts well and that she is certain about what she can offer. At the same time, Zoe is neither boastful nor over confident. Therefore, she confines her responses to the topic at hand rather than going into too much detail about her life story. When it comes to the inevitable question of discussing her weaknesses, Zoe limits her story to telling the essentials and the lessons she has learned from these experiences. She has a positive perspective about her weaknesses, indicating a healthy self-awareness and a recognition of the value of her experiences.

Zoe also knows that body language speaks volumes and is well-versed in assessing her own body language. Zoe practises yoga which means that to a certain extent she is familiar with the concept of power poses. Remember Amy Cuddy from Chapter 8? Amy Cuddy's recent research with Caroline Wilmuth and Dana Carney tests power posing in a real, high-impact social situation: a job interview.

The research picture

The current experiment tested whether changing one's nonverbal behaviour prior to a high-stakes social evaluation could improve performance in the evaluated task. Participants adopted expansive, open (high-power) poses, or contractive, closed (low-power) poses, and then prepared and delivered a speech to two evaluators as part of a mock job interview, a prototypical social evaluation. All speeches were videotaped and coded for overall performance and hirability, and the potential mediators of speech quality (e.g., content, structure) and presentation quality (e.g., captivating, confident). As predicted, high power posers performed better and were more likely to be chosen for hire, and this relationship was mediated only by presentation quality, not speech quality. Power pose condition had no effect on body posture during the social evaluation, thus highlighting the relationship between *preparatory* nonverbal behaviour and *subsequent* performance. (Cuddy et al., 2012, p. 2)

Beyond a person simply performing better in the interview, the research found that adopting the power pose had an effect on cortisol and testosterone levels. High power pose people showed a 20% increase in testosterone (the dominance hormone) and a 25% decrease in cortisol (the stress hormone).

Before the interview Zoe actually did pop to the ladies and did a couple of quick power poses which immediately increased the levels of testosterone into her body, pumping her for the interview, calming any nerves and releasing positive energy.

During the interview Zoe avoids slouching and maintains her composure. Her body itself is in an open stance, she maintains eye contact. Although she does feel herself tensing up a little as the interview starts, she is aware of this. She accepts the offer of a glass of water, takes some deep breaths and a couple of seconds to centre herself and to really be in the present moment. She knows that one of the most important skills she can draw on during an interview is active listening. So she is aware of the need for empathy, recognising that the interviewer may have concerns that they do a good job of interviewing and may well feel under pressure themselves.

Because Zoe has prepared for the interview so well, she is able to interact in the moment feeling confident and secure in her responses and approaches to the questions posed. She also has questions herself and is engaged and interesting as well as interested. None of this has required enormous effort on Zoe's part *during the interview itself* aside from being able to relax and be in the present moment.

A number of outcomes are possible here: Zoe may or may not get the job. She may decide after the interview and on reflection that this is not the right role for her and equally the interviewer may decide that even though Zoe interviews so well, that she is possibly better suited to a different position. Or Zoe gets the job but they want an immediate start. Or they can't open up the role for another two months. The point here is that whatever the outcome Zoe feels good about it and is able to move on to the next challenge, whether starting the job or renewing her search armed with what she has learned from this interview process. She leaves the interview and feels good about the day ahead.

Zoe gets the job

Now, let's imagine Zoe did get the job and we are with her during her working week. She is a junior digital projects manager for a media company. Her role involves analysing client requirements, establishing the scope and deliverables of a project and working with the development team to create project milestones. Zoe also has to write proposals and generate sitemaps and other specification documentation. Within the course of her work Zoe interacts with external designers, ensuring designs are produced on time and on budget. She has to work closely with her own project team, managing them accordingly, which means regular meetings and updates. Zoe also has to train clients on how to use their content management systems and help with supporting existing websites, both in terms of bugs and new work packages. The role requires strong communication and leadership skills, and a desire to learn, problem solve and learn new processes quickly.

In a typical working week Zoe might deal with the following types of communication:

- Composing and responding to internal and external emails
- Giving a sales presentation to a prospective client

- Providing a report on current design projects for the quarter at the monthly management meeting
- Attending a conference and networking event
- Responding to telephone calls about a problem with a website
- Making a series of calls to research different content management systems and support packages
- Internal instant messaging
- Taking part in a team meeting
- Leading the development team
- Video and audio conferencing.

Because Zoe does not operate only in connection to her work it's also important to take a holistic view of her life. Being able to function at optimum levels within our communication requires an awareness of other aspects of our lives that impact this and knowing how to look after ourselves in order to make a maximum difference.

So let's take a quick look at Zoe's weekend.

Zoe's weekend: Take 1

Zoe believes that weekends are all about relaxing – after all, she works very hard. She spends most of the weekend going out with friends, although she does fit in some time for cycling and a movie. On Saturday Zoe is a bit annoyed about a silly misunderstanding with her flatmate about leaving a mess in the kitchen. She can't see what 'all the fuss is about' and thinks her flatmate is too particular. She doesn't need this kind of stress on the weekend! Zoe, being a bit of a hothead, ends up slamming the door on her way out for the evening and deciding that she really does deserve a good night out now!

She hardly thinks about work at all until Sunday evening when she makes a quick list of some ideas she has had for a new way of managing projects. Zoe doesn't manage to resolve things with her flatmate as she doesn't feel she has 'done anything wrong'. She still feels a bit annoyed and posts a comment on her social media feed about it and immediately feels better when she gets validation from her friends about her actions.

Zoe's weekend: Take 2

During her weekend Zoe is out with friends and has a late night on Saturday. Before she goes out, Zoe's flatmate approaches her about some mess that Zoe had left in the kitchen the day before. Zoe feels annoyed but also knows that choosing to get upset about the situation is not going to be productive. She takes some deep breaths and then sits down with her flatmate and listens to her concerns accepting that, for whatever reason, mess matters to her. Zoe apologises, clears up the mess and leaves for the evening. Zoe has used cognitive behavioural techniques (CBT) (Chapter 1 – *Your Amazing Brain*) to reframe the way she was looking at the situation.

Zoe then spends a relaxed Sunday afternoon planning her week. Zoe knows about the power of writing things down and planning ahead (Chapter 9 – *The Power of the Pen*) and wants to start the week with high energy. She uses a planner which includes space for reflection notes as well as for prioritising her day. The week is busy with a number of presentations and meetings and Zoe knows that there will also be additional things that she might not be able to plan ahead for. So she works on the areas she has control over and makes sure that she has factored in preparation time as well as time for important conversations and ensuring that her communications are clear. Zoe also plans in regular exercise during the week as well as working out when she will shop for groceries and cook healthy meals. She schedules a couple of evenings for meeting friends and relaxing too.

Now we will take a look at Zoe's Monday through two takes:

Monday: Take 1

Zoe has an overload of emails first thing and she starts looking at these on the train to work – things have piled up. Once she gets into work she immediately spends the first two hours of the day responding to her emails. This is using up vital brain energy that she needs for more high-level work (Chapter 2 – *Overcoming Distraction* and Chapter 3 – *Working Smarter*).

An unexpected meeting comes up late morning and means Zoe is not able to prepare for the mid-week meeting as she had hoped which starts to trigger stress for her – she starts worrying about why this meeting has been called and what is going to happen. As a consequence, Zoe does not pay as much attention to what is happening during the meeting as she should. Like others during the meeting she looks at her phone from time to time to 'keep on top of' her messages. So Zoe is paying attention to parts of the meeting but because she is distracted she isn't fully present and therefore is not actively listening to what is going on around her. So she misses some vital cues about an issue that might have benefited from some of her ideas and that it might have been important for her to be alert to for all sorts of reasons (Chapter 6 – *Meetings, Presentations and Networking*).

Zoe grabs a quick lunch on the go and gets back into planning for the mid-week meeting but is quickly distracted by more emails and by colleagues checking in with her about various things. It's difficult to get into the planning so she leaves it for now and decides to start on something else but still has to work through distractions.

Later that afternoon she calls a team meeting which is needed to prepare for the latest project – she rings but can't get hold of anyone and feels frustrated which then results in a badly written and unclear email requiring lots of checking by the team. Zoe realises that perhaps it would have been better to use messaging or her project management system to coordinate the meeting as well as post up some documents that it is vital for the team to be aware of (Chapter 4 – *Effective Email*, Chapter 8 – *Using the Telephone* and Chapter 9 – *Online Meetings and Conferences*).

Finally, in the late afternoon Zoe realises she is behind on preparing for the mid-week meeting and so spends some time at the end of the day putting some quick notes together before leaving for the evening. On her way home she again goes through emails and answers a few.

Monday: Take 2

First of all, Zoe starts the day (and every day) with a healthy breakfast full of brain-nurturing foods. She also packs a healthy lunch to take with her. Zoe is aware that she is likely to have a lot of emails to check through but resists the urge to do this on the morning commute. Instead she catches up on a podcast about project management tools and puts together her thoughts and ideas for the mid-week meeting, making sure she sets a reminder to send through an agenda that afternoon.

Zoe arrives at work. She flips through her planner, noting what she has scheduled for the day and ticking off on her list her preparation task for the mid-week meeting. Zoe has a good relationship with her colleagues and a healthy network of support around her. As a result she is fairly resilient.

She uses her project management software to call a development team meeting for the end of the week, invites team members to flag up areas they want to address and creates a central point to post meeting documents related to the project. Zoe then sets reminders to check in to the platform in two days' time to ensure all the documentation is ready. Unexpectedly, Zoe gets called into an urgent meeting just when she was about to start going through her email. She quickly scans her inbox and only looks at the most important emails related to current clients. Zoe's email system is set up into folders and is filtered project by project which means that anything that is not immediate is put into a different folder which she can go through later. Zoe sets flags against the four emails she needs to respond to that day and goes into the meeting. Because it is unusual to be called to a meeting at such short notice Zoe is aware that she needs to pay close attention. She switches her phone to mute, takes a few deep breaths to centre herself and walks into the meeting with her notepad and pen. During the meeting Zoe is observant of body language and the general atmosphere, notes the tension and listens carefully. As a result she is able to contribute some useful ideas to help the situation.

Once back at her desk, Zoe responds to the four emails from clients. Meanwhile, some other emails have come through which she quickly sorts, flagging up those that she needs to respond to today and others that can wait.

Zoe then takes a break, gets outside for a walk and for lunch returning to the office refreshed and ready for the afternoon. She starts working on a report for one of the company's latest clients. A phone call comes through from a potential new client. Zoe takes the call, asks a few questions and then arranges a time later that week when they can go into the project in more depth, making a note to research some of the key areas the client wants to explore. Zoe finishes the report and then takes a break which gives her the opportunity to catch up with a few colleagues.

Towards the end of the day Zoe checks into the company internal messaging system, responding to a few points and flagging up some new discussion areas on one of the collaboration team boards she has started. Before she leaves for the day Zoe clears her desk, checks her email once more – this time clearing the folders of any unneeded emails and noting any new emails which will require a response in the next two days.

Zoe leaves the office after a productive day, attends a yoga class and returns home to cook and have a relaxing evening. On the train on the way home she takes out her planner and reviews the day, noting what has gone well and what she could have handled differently. She then makes some notes for tasks to attend to the following day and starts listening to some music.

The rest of the week: Take 1

If we continue where we left off on Take 1 for Monday we will find that everything overlaps. Maybe Zoe is now worried about leading the team because the email communication has been so ineffective. She leaves for work without breakfast as she is in a hurry to get stuff done. This has an impact because her brain needs and is not getting the vital nutrients it needs for Zoe to function effectively in her job. Not having breakfast also results in Zoe drinking too much coffee. Zoe feels and believes that she should be able to deal with things by herself so generally she does not call on anyone for help and has no real strong network of support around her. This means Zoe is less able to deal with the unexpected. Perhaps on one of the weekday evenings Zoe has to go the networking event and hasn't prepared. She doesn't feel confident, starts to worry, and then misses out on important cues when networking and talking to people. Consequently Zoe gets a headache and feels overwhelmed which causes her to sleep badly that night.

When Zoe gets to the mid-week meeting she is not prepared and therefore stays up late the night before to get her presentation ready. This is not the best time to do this because preparing this late may trigger worry and stress in Zoe's brain, especially as giving presentations tends to be stressful anyway.

Zoe continues to deal with emails first thing in the morning and as and when they come in which causes numerous interruptions to her day. She does not tend to plan ahead sufficiently to feel relaxed and ready for the important events (i.e. the networking event, the team meeting) and is ill-equipped to handle unexpected meetings and calls which are inevitable in the course of a working week. Throughout the week pressure continues to pile up, causing Zoe to feel overwhelmed and not in control. Although she is able to gather herself and rally through, the lack of planning and reflection time impacts her. So when, for example, her boss asks for an update on the networking event she attended this causes yet more stress and tension. She had not been in touch with him about this at all and because it did not go well she feels flustered and does not respond as effectively as she would have liked. She in turn misinterprets the response of her boss and feels upset for the rest of the day. This then continues into the mid-week presentation when she stumbles over her talk; she doesn't like giving presentations at the best of times and all her fears kick into gear because of the way she is feeling anyway.

It is clear to see the spiral of events here. If we continued we would find out that Zoe responds badly to a phone call about a website problem because it comes on top of the other pressures and even though she is fully competent to deal with the issue this competence does not shine through as it could do because her telephone manner is abrupt (due to feeling stressed). When she is asked to lead the video conference she is unfamiliar with the software because she did not have time to familiarise herself with the video tutorials. This results in an inefficient meeting.

The rest of the week: Take 2

Just like in Take 1, the way we live out a day overlaps and has an impact on the day following it. For Zoe eating breakfast and having time for a swim might be a normal way to begin a day. She is more likely to be familiar with and use the project management system with her team so she might use it to post an amusing video or something that helps with team cohesion. She will more likely call on her network for support and this also helps her team to work together well and communicate well. She will take time to think about the networking event and what she will do there so that she is sure to make real and strong connections with people. Maybe she also checks in with her boss to see how she can add value and contribute when she goes to the event. After the event, Zoe will spend some time reflecting, writing up some notes and some ideas for follow-up.

Zoe does not allow email to sap her energy and take her away from her work so she uses filtering systems and folders and is not 'always on'. This isn't always easy and it's not that Zoe isn't tempted to check her emails and messages but more that she recognises her brain's natural compulsion to want to do this and has found ways to override it which immediately gives her more space and planning time.

The purpose of looking at Zoe's week in this way is to simply highlight examples of where communication processes are not as effective as they could be and the ripple effect this has on Zoe's productivity levels, her relationships, her stress and happiness levels and ultimately on her work and wellbeing. It is unlikely that Zoe would experience all of this in one week and it is actually far more likely that Take 1 situations are mixed with Take 2 situations for each of us. It is equally likely that we will continue to experience a mix of Take 1 and Take 2. With awareness, though, we can lessen the possibilities of Take 1 and function more in Take 2 where our potential and our talents lie and where our true ability to communicate and function effectively reside.

It is worth reiterating here that everything really does begin with your own self-awareness – self-awareness about how you are living your life, how you are choosing to respond to stress and what triggers stress for you, and self-awareness about how you communicate.

This is also why so many of the exercises in this book recommend that you try things out, reflect and write things down (by hand!). It is not so much about using specific templates and methods, though these are important, but about really thinking through your own communication skills in different settings, why you do what you do, how you can approach something differently and can as a result be a stronger and more successful communicator.

Bibliography – chapter by chapter

Introduction

David, D. & Foray, D. 2002. An introduction to the economy of the knowledge society. *International Social Science Journal*, 54(171), 9–23.

Halford, S. 2015. *Activate Your Brain: How Understanding Your Brain Can Improve Your Work – and Your Life*. Austin, TX: Greenleaf Book Group Press.

Lebwohl, B. 2011, 10 February. Martin Hilbert: All human information, stored on CD, would reach beyond the moon. *EarthSky*. Available at: http://foresightculture.com/2015/07/02/the-best-time-in-history [Accessed 20 February 2017].

Mahaffie, J. B. 2015, 15 July. The best time in history. Available at: http://foresightculture.com/2015/07/02/the-best-time-in-history [Accessed 20 February 2017].

Chapter 1 – Your Amazing Brain

Arnsten, A. F. T. 1998. The biology of being frazzled. *Science*, 280, 1711–1712.

Barnlund, 1970. A transactional model of communication. In K. K. Sereno & C. D. Mortensen (Eds), *Foundations of Communication Theory* (pp. 83–102). New York: Harper & Row.

Berlo, D. 1960. *The Process of Communication*. New York: Holt, Rinehart, & Winston.

Goldin P. R., Gross J. J. 2010. Effects of mindfulness-based stress reduction (MBSR) on emotion regulation in social anxiety disorder. *Emotion*, 10(1), 83–91.

Goldin, P. R. & Gross, J. J. 2014. Effects of mindfulness-based stress reduction (MBSR) on emotion regulation in social anxiety disorder. *Behaviour Research & Therapy*, 56, 7–15.

Goleman, D. n. d. *Emotional Intelligence*. [online] Available at: www.danielgoleman.info/topics/emotional-intelligence [Accessed 29 June 2016].

Goleman, D. 1996. *Emotional Intelligence: Why it Can Matter More Than IQ*. London: Bloomsbury Publishing.

Goleman, D. 1999. *Working with Emotional Intelligence*. London: Bloomsbury Publishing.

Goleman, D. 2003. *The New Leaders: Transforming the Art of Leadership*. London: Sphere Publishing.

Hollon, S. D. & Beck, A. T. 1994. Cognitive and cognitive-behavioral therapies. In A. E. Bergin & S. L. Garfield (Eds), *Handbook of Psychotherapy and Behavior Change* (pp. 428–466). New York: Wiley.

Lanham, R.A. 2007. *The Economics of Attention: Style and Substance in the Age of Information*. University of Chicago Press.

Lieberman, M. D., Eisenberger, N. I., Crockett, M. J., Tom, S., Pfeifer, J. H., Way, B. M. (2007). Putting feelings into words: Affect labeling disrupts amygdala activity to affective stimuli. *Psychological Science*, 18, 421–428.

Ochsner, K. N. & Gross, J. J. 2005. The cognitive control of emotion. *Trends in Cognitive Sciences*, 9(5), 242–249.

Rock, D. n. d. About. Available at: http://davidrock.net/about/ [Accessed 28 July 2016].

Rock, D. 2008. SCARF: A brain-based model for collaborating with and influencing others. *NeuroLeadership Journal*, 1, 44–52.

Schramm, W. 1964. *Mass Media and National Development: The Role of Information in the Developing Countries*. Stanford, California: Stanford University Press.

Shannon, C. 1948. A mathematical theory of communication. *Bell System Technical Journal*, 27 (July and October), 379–423, 623–656.

Torrisi, S. J., Lieberman, M. D., Bookheimer, S. Y. & Altshuler, L. L. 2013. Advancing understanding of affect labeling with dynamic causal modeling. *NeuroImage*, 82, 481–488.

Weaver, W. & Shannon, C. E. 1963. *The Mathematical Theory of Communication*. University of Illinois Press.

Chapter 2 – How to Overcome Distraction

Allelyne, R. 2011, 11 February. Welcome to the information age – 75 newspapers a day. *The Telegraph*.

Bland, A. 2013. Driven to distraction: Have we lost the ability to focus on a single task? *The Independent*. Available at: www.independent.co.uk/arts-entertainment/books/features/driven-to-distraction-have-we-lost-the-ability-to-focus-on-a-single-task-8914010.html [Accessed 20 February 2017].

Bohn, R. E. & Short, J. E. 2011. How much information? 2011 report on American consumers. *Global Information Industry Centre Report*.

Broadbent, D. 1958. *Perception and Communication*. London: Pergamon Press.

Ekman, P. 2007. *Emotions Revealed, Second Edition: Recognizing Faces and Feelings to Improve Communication and Emotional Life*. New York: Holt.

Friedenberg, J. & Silverman, G. 2012. *Cognitive Science: An Introduction to the Study of Mind*. Los Angeles, CA: Sage Publications.

Gathercole, S. E. & Packiam, T. 2012. *A Guide to Working Memory*. Alloway: University of York.

Globerson, T. 1983. Mental capacity, mental effort, and cognitive style. *Developmental Review*, 3, 292–302.

Halford, Scott D. 2015. *Activate Your Brain: How Understanding Your Brain Can Improve Your Work – and Your Life*. Austin, TX: Greenleaf Book Group Press.

Hardy, Q. 2014, 8 January. Today's webcams see all (tortoise we're watching your back). *New York Times*, p. A1.

Lyman, P., Varian, H. R., Swearingen, K., Charles, P., Good, N., Jordan, L. L. & Pal, J. 2003. How much information? *University of California at Berkeley School of Information Management Report*.

Mark, G. 2016. *The Cost of Interrupted Work: More Speed and Stress*. Irvine, CA: Department of Informatics at the University of California.

Masley, S., Roetzheim, R. & Gualtieri, T. 2009. Aerobic exercise enhances cognitive flexibility. *Journal of Clinical Psychology in Medical Settings*, 16(2), 186–193. doi:10.1007/s10880-009-9159-6 (2009 Jun).

McLeod, S. A. 2008. Simply Psychology. [online] Available at: www.simplypsychology.org/attention-models.html [Accessed 1 July 2016].

Nunberg, G. 2001, 20 March. James Glieck's history of information. *The New York Sunday Book Review*, p. BR1.

Pink, D. 2011. *A Whole New Mind. Why Right-Brainers Will Rule the Future*. Marshall Cavendish. [online] Available at: www.danpink.com/books/whole-new-mind [Accessed 30 June 2016].

The Salt. 2015, 31 August. *If Fish is Brain Food, Can Fish Oil Pills Boost Brains Too?* [online] Available at: www.npr.org/sections/thesalt/2015/08/31/435264223/if-fish-is-brain-food-can-fish-oil-pills-boost-brains-too [Accessed 1 July 2016].

Walker, M. P., Liston, C. J., Hobson, A. & Stickgold, R. 2002, March. Cognitive flexibility across the sleep–wake cycle: REM-sleep enhancement of anagram problem solving. *Cognitive Brain Research*, 14, 317–324. Research report. [online] Available at: https://walkerlab.berkeley. edu/reprints/Walkeretal_CogBrainRes_2002.pdf [Accessed 27 July 2016].

Chapter 3 – Working Smarter

Baumeister, R. F. & Tierney, J. 2012. *Willpower: Why Self-Control is The Secret to Success.* London: Penguin.

Baumeister, R. F., Schmeichel, B. J. & Vohs, K. D. 2003. Intellectual performance and ego depletion: Role of the self in logical reasoning and other information processing. *Journal of Personality and Social Psychology*, 85(1), 33–46. doi:10.1037/0022-3514.85.1.33.

Dweck, C. S. 2007. *Mindset: The New Psychology of Success – How We Can Learn to Fulfil Our Potential.* New York: Ballantine.

Ernst, A. & Frisén, J. 2015, January. Adult neurogenesis in humans – common and unique traits in mammals. *PLoS Biology*, 13(1), e1002045.

Gailliot, M. T., Baumeister, R. F., DeWall, C. N., Maner, J. K., Plant, E. A., Tice, D. M., Brewer, L. E. & Schmeichel, B. J. 2007. Self-control relies on glucose as a limited energy source: Willpower is more than a metaphor. *Journal of Personality and Social Psychology*, 92(2), 325.

Harter, J. K., Schmidt, F. L., Killham, E. A. & Agrawal, S. T. L. 2009. Q12® Meta-Analysis: The Relationship Between Engagement at Work and Organisational Outcomes. [online] Available at: www.gallup.com/consulting/File/126806/MetaAnalysis_Q12_WhitePaper_2009.pdf [Accessed 5 June 2011].

Kessler, R. C., Berglund, P. A., Coulouvrat, C., Hajak, G., Roth, T., Shahly, V., Shillington, A. C., Stephenson, J. J. & Walsh, J. K. 2011. Insomnia and the performance of US workers: Results from the America Insomnia Survey. *Sleep*, 34(9), 1161–1171.

Ming, G. L. & Song, H. 2011. Adult neurogenesis in the mammalian brain: Significant answers and significant questions. *Neuron*, 70(4), 687–702.

Steel, P. 2007. The nature of procrastination: A meta-analytic and theoretical review of quintessential self-regulatory failure. *Psychological Bulletin*, 133(1), 65–94.

Chapter 4 – Effective Email

Barton, E. 2015, 14 January. *Love It or Loathe It, Email Changed the World.* [online] Available at: www.bbc.com/capital/story/20150109-love-it-or-loathe-it-email-changede-the-world?icid=cap.aut.sto.cross-site-series.bc.turning-points_week2 [Accessed 29 July 2016].

Berridge, K. C. & Robinson, T. E. 1998. What is the role of dopamine in reward: Hedonic impact, reward learning, or incentive salience? *Brain Research Reviews*, 28, 309–369.

Derks, D. & Bakker, A. 2010. The impact of e-mail communication on organizational life. *Cyberpsychology: Journal of Psychosocial Research on Cyberspace*, 4(1), article 1. Available at: http://cyberpsychology.eu/view.php?cisloclanku=2010052401&article=1 [Accessed 20 February 2017].

Kushlev, K. & Dunn, E. W. 2015. Checking email less frequently reduces stress. *Computer in Human Behavior*, 43 (February), 220–228.

Le Merrer, J., Becker, J. A. J., Befort, K. & Kieffer, B. L. 2009. Reward processing by the opioid system in the brain. *Physiological Reviews*, 89(4), 1379–1412. doi:10.1152/ physrev.00005.2009 (Oct).

Lee, Y. K., Chang, C. T., Lin, Y. & Cheng, Z. H. 2014. The dark side of smartphone usage: Psychological traits, compulsive behavior and technostress. *Computers in Human Behavior*, 31, 373–383.

McKenna, K. Y. A. & Bargh, J. A. 2000. Plan 9 from cyberspace: The implications of the Internet for personality and social psychology. *Personality and Social Psychology Bulletin*, 4, 57–75.

Radicati Group. n. d. Email Statistics Report, 2015–2019. [online] Available at: www.radicati.com/wp/wp-content/uploads/2015/02/Email-Statistics-Report-2015-2 019-Executive-Summary.pdf [Accessed 20 February 2017].

Skapinker, M. 2013, 26 June. Does it matter if students can't write? *Financial Times*.

Vanhemert, K. 2015, 24 April. *Write the Perfect Email to Anyone with This Creepy Site*. [online] Available at: www.wired.com/2015/04/write-perfect-email-anyone-creepy-site/ [Accessed 29 July 2016].

Chapter 5 – Face-to-Face Communication

Gloor, P. A., Grippa, F., Lassenius, C., Putzke, J., Fuehres, H., Schoder, D. & Fischbach, K. 2012. Measuring social capital in creative teams through sociometric sensors. *International Journal of Organisational Design and Engineering*, 2(4), 380–401.

Harvard Business Review. 2009. *Managing Across Distance in Today's Economic Climate: The Value of Face-to-Face Communication*. [pdf] Available at: https://hbr.org/resources/pdfs/comm/british-airways/hbras_ba_report_web.pdf [Accessed 1 July 2016].

Higgins, M. 2014, 10 March. *Using the STAR Technique to Shine at Job Interviews: A How-to Guide*. [online] Available at: www.theguardian.com/careers/careers-blog/star-techniqu e-competency-based-interview [Accessed 29 July 2016].

Jiang, J., Dai, B., Peng, D., Zhu, C, Liu, L. & Lu, C. 2012. Neural synchronization during face-to-face communication. *The Journal of Neuroscience*, 32(45), 16064–16069. doi:10.1523/JNEUROSCI.2926-12.2012.

Mehrabian, A. & Wiener, M. 1967, May. Decoding of inconsistent communications. *Journal of Personality and Social Psychology*, 6(1), 109–114. [online] Available at: http://dx.doi.org/10.1037/h0024532 [Accessed 1 July 2016].

Pentland, A. 2012. *The New Science of Building Great Teams*. [online] Available at: https://hbr.org/2012/04/the-new-science-of-building-great-teams [Accessed 29 July 2016].

Pink, D. 2011. *A Whole New Mind. Why Right-Brainers Will Rule the Future*. Marshall Cavendish. [online] Available at: www.danpink.com/books/whole-new-mind [Accessed 30 June 2016].

Princeton University Institute. 2014. *Uri Hasson*. [online] Available at: https://pni.princeton.edu/faculty/uri-hasson [Accessed 1 July 2016].

Stern, C. 2016, 3 March. *The Ultimate Working Lunch: Inside the Envy-inducing Canteens of Companies Like Dropbox, Google and Pixar that Offer Free Food, Extensive Menus and Gourmet Desserts*. [online] Available at: www.dailymail.co.uk/femail/article-3473854/The-ULTIMATE-working-lunch-Inside-envy-inducing-canteens-companies-like-Dropbox-Google-Pixar-offer-free-food-extensive-menus-gourmet-desserts.html [Accessed 1 July 2016].

Swisher, K. 'Physically together': Here's the internal Yahoo no-work-from-home memo for remote workers and maybe more [online]. Available at: http://allthingsd.com/20130222/physically-together-heres-the-internal-yahoo-no-work-from-home-memo-which-extend s-beyond-remote-workers/ [Accessed 20 February 2017].

Tkaczyk, C. 2013, 13 April. *Marissa Mayer Breaks Her Silence on Yahoo's Telecommuting Policy*. [online] Available at: http://fortune.com/2013/04/19/marissa-mayer-breaks-her-silenc e-on-yahoos-telecommuting-policy/ [Accessed 20 February 2017].

Chapter 6 – Meetings, Presentations and Networking

GlassDoor. 2016. *GlassDoor for Employers, 50 HR and Recruiting Stats That Make You Think*. Available at: https://b2b-assets.glassdoor.com/50-hr-and-recruiting-stats.pdf. [Accessed November 2016].

McClafferty, A. 2015. *12 'Fear of Public Speaking' Symptoms and How to Beat Them. Forbes.* [online] Available at: www.forbes.com/sites/alexmcclafferty/2015/01/12/ fear-of-public-speaking [Accessed 30 January 2017].

Chapter 7 – Getting Social Media Right

Asae, L. & Dosemagen, S. 2016. *How Social Media is Shaking Up Healthcare. World Economic Forum.* [online] Available at: www.weforum.org/agenda/2016/04/how-social-media-is-shaking-up-healthcare [Accessed 2 July 2016].

CDAC Network. 2016. *The International Network of Crisis Mappers.* [online] Available at: www. cdacnetwork.org/marketplace/service-directory/i/20140609182929-hctaa [Accessed 2 July 2016].

Chaykowski, K. 2016. *Facebook Safety Check Glitch Asks Users Far from Lahore Pakistan if They are Safe After Explosion. Forbes.* [online] Available at: www.forbes.com/sites/ kathleenchaykowski/2016/03/27/facebook-safety-check-glitch-asks-users-far-from-lahore-pakistan-if-they-are-safe-after-explosion/#5318fea21585 [Accessed 2 July 2016].

Eldridge, R. 2016. *How Social Media is Shaping Financial Services. World Economic Forum.* [online] Available at: www.weforum.org/agenda/2016/04/how-social-media-is-shaping-financial-services [Accessed 2 July 2016].

Griffith, E. 2016. *Facebook Video is Huge and Growing Like Crazy. Fortune.* [online] Available at: http://fortune.com/2015/11/04/facebook-video-growth/ [Accessed 2 July 2016].

Guo, E. 2016. *5 Ways Social Media is Changing Business as Usual for Governments. World Economic Forum.* [online] Available at: www.weforum.org/agenda/2016/04/5-ways-social-media-is-changing-business-as-usual-for-governments [Accessed 2 July 2016].

Guzman, A. & Vis, F. 7 April 2016. *6 Ways Social Media is Changing the World. World Economic Forum.* [online] Available at: www.weforum.org/agenda/2016/04/6-ways-social-media-is-changing-the-world [Accessed 29 July 2016].

IBM 2010 *Global CEO Study: Creativity Selected as Most Crucial Factor for Future Success.* Available at: www-03.ibm.com/press/us/en/pressrelease/31670.wss [Accessed November 2016].

Leson, H. 2016. *How is Social Media Helping Disaster Response. World Economic Forum.* [online] Available at: www.weforum.org/agenda/2016/04/how-is-social-media-helping-disaster-response [Accessed 2 July 2016].

Statista 2016. *Number of Social Network Users Worldwide from 2010 to 2019 (in billions).* [online] Available at: www.statista.com/statistics/278414/number-of-worldwide-social-network-users [Accessed 2 July 2016].

Wardle, C. 2016. *Is this the Biggest Disruptor of the News Industry? World Economic Forum.* [online] Available at: www.weforum.org/agenda/2016/04/is-this-the-biggest-disruptor-of-the-news-industry [Accessed 2 July 2016].

World Economic Forum. 2016. *Global Agenda on Council on Social Media.* [online] Available at: www.weforum.org/communities/global-agenda-council-on-social-media [Accessed 2 July 2016].

Chapter 8 – Using the Telephone

Deloitte. 2015. Mobile Consumer 2015: The UK cut. *Game of Phones* [pdf] Available at: www. deloitte.co.uk/mobileuk [Accessed 29 July 2016].

Paul, P. 2011, 18 March. *Don't Call Me, I Won't Call You. New York Times.* [online]. Available at: www.nytimes.com/2011/03/20/fashion/20Cultural.html?pagewanted=all&_r=1 [Accessed 29 July 2016].

Son, H. 2015, 2 June. *JP Morgan Kills Voice Mail. Bloomberg* [online]. Available at: www. bloomberg.com/news/articles/2015-06-02/jpmorgan-says-don-t-leave-message-at-the-tone-as-voice-mail-dies [Accessed 29 July 2016].

Chapter 9 – Online Meetings and Conferences

Absalom, R. & Drury, A. 2014. *Ovum 2.0 – The Death of Web Conferencing (as we know it)*. [pdf] Available at: www.logmeininc.com/~/media/5d4d2ef5287d4301935f67903bf3b18d.pdf [Accessed 29 July 2016].

Ale Ebrahim, N., Ahmed, S. & Taha, Z. 2009. Virtual teams: A literature review. *Australian Journal of Basic and Applied Sciences*, 3(3), 2653–2669.

Dolby Voice. 2014. Why you hate conference calls. Available at: https://blog.dolby.com/2014/03/why-you-hate-conference-calls/ [Accessed 20 February 2017].

The Economist, Economist Intelligence Unit. 2009. *Managing Virtual Teams: Taking a More Strategic Approach*. [pdf] Available at: http://graphics.eiu.com/upload/eb/NEC_Managing_virtual_teams_WEB.pdf. [Accessed 29 July 2016].

Hastings, R. (July 1, 2010). Fostering Virtual Working Relationships Isn't Easy. SHRM Online. Retrieved 15th March 2017 from http://www.shrm.org.

RW³. 2010. *The Challenges of Working in Virtual Teams*. Virtual Teams Survey Report. [pdf] Available at: www.communicationcache.com/uploads/1/0/8/8/10887248/the_challenges_of_working_in_virtual_teams.pdf [Accessed 29 July 2016].

Chapter 10 – The Power of the Pen

Cameron, J. 1995. *The Artist's Way: A Course in Discovering and Recovering Your Creative Self*. Pan.

Capacchione, Lucia. 2000. *The Power of Your Other Hand,* 2nd ed. Franklin Lakes, NJ: New Page Books.

Huffington, Arianna. 2015. *Thrive: The Third Metric to Redefining Success and Creating a Happier Life*. London: W. H. Allen.

Klauser, Henriette, A. 2001. *Write It Down Make It Happen: Knowing What You Want and Getting It!* Simon & Schuster.

MacManus, Chris. 2003. *Right Hand, Left Hand*. London: W&N.

Mueller, P. A. & Oppenheimer, D. M. 2014. *The Pen is Mightier than the Keyboard: Advantages of Longhand Over Laptop Note Taking*. Los Angeles: Princeton University, University of California.

National Pens Company. 2016. *What Does Your Handwriting Say About You?* [online]. Available at: www.pens.com/handwriting-infographic. [Accessed 29 July 2016].

PayScale. 2016. *Leveling Up: How to Win in the Skills Economy*. [online] Available at: www.payscale.com/data-packages/job-skills [Accessed 20 February 2017].

Chapter 11 – Putting it All Together

Cuddy. A. J. C., Wilmuth, C. A. & Carney, D. R. 2012. *The Benefit of Power Posing Before a High-Stakes Evaluation*. [online] Available at: https://dash.harvard.edu/bitstream/handle/1/9547823/13-027.pdf?sequence=1 [Accessed on 20 February 2017].

Index